SAVOR *Seattle*

RECIPES FROM SEATTLE'S TOP RESTAURANTS
PAIRED WITH WINES FROM THE NORTHWEST'S BEST WINERIES

ELIZABETH ALAIN

ELTON-WOLF PUBLISHING

Featuring food photography by Kate Baldwin
Featuring photograph scans by Seattle Imagesetting, Inc.

Cover design by Jeanne Hendrickson, Hendrickson Design
Text design & layout by Jeanne Hendrickson, Hendrickson Design

Published by Elton-Wolf Publishing
Seattle, Washington

Books can be purchased through: www.Elton-wolf.com

Recipes, including ingredients and measurements, have been provided by the restaurants and developed for use in this book. The publisher does not take responsibility for the accuracy of the recipes or the results of the preparation or consumption of the recipes.

ISBN: 1-58619-105-5
Library of Congress Card Catalog Number: 2004110222
08 07 06 05 04   1 2 3 4 5

First Edition October 2004

Printed in Korea
Amica International, Inc.

Other Savor Series books (to be released 2005/2006)
Savor San Francisco
Savor New Orleans
Savor Montreal
Savor Beijing

ELTON-WOLF PUBLISHING
2505 Second Avenue Suite 515 Seattle, Washington 98121
Tel 206.748.0345 Fax 206.748.0343
www.elton-wolf.com info@elton-wolf.com

CONTENTS

Known for its Space Needle, ferries, mountains, water, airplanes, and technology, Seattle has stepped into the 21st century with some of the finest dining and the best wines in the world.

Where else can you dine on the water with a spectacular view of Seattle and finish up with a ball game at a state-of-the-art baseball field; enjoy the fragrance of herbs in a garden that later adorn your plate; relax after a day of skiing or sailing with a plate of salmon in front of a river rock fireplace; take in a world class play and finish with a late night dinner with food to rival any you'll find anywhere in the world?

The best of Seattle's kitchens and the Northwest's harvests can now be enjoyed in your home.

This book is dedicated to Seattle and all those who make it what it is.

Savor Seattle!

Publisher

Lamont Jacobsen

WHO PLANTED THE SEED AND BROUGHT IN THE HARVEST

The restaurants and wineries

WHO AGREED TO SHARE THEIR BEST SO WE CAN ENJOY
THEIR BEST IN OUR HOMES

Eileen Mintz

WHO LENT HER UNWAVERING SUPPORT THROUGHOUT
THE PROJECT

Jeanne Hendrickson

WHO BLESSED THE PROJECT WITH HER GIFT OF STYLE
AND DESIGN

Colleen Christensen

WHO USED HER WORD CRAFT TO BRING THE ATMOSPHERE
OF THE RESTAURANTS TO LIFE IN PRINT

XII

Brooke Farrell, Kylee Krida, Ryan Danis

WHO LENT THEIR EYES TO THE DETAILS

Elton Welke

WHO MAKES ALL THINGS POSSIBLE

Gamberoni alla Griglia

Insalata di Panzanella

Linguine alla Mauro

Porchetta Ripiene al Portobello

Tiramisu

Assaggio

ASSAGGIO RISTORANTE
MAURO GOLMARVI,
OWNER

2010 FOURTH AVENUE

SEATTLE, WA 98121

206.441.1399

www.assaggioseattle.com

WALKING INTO ASSAGGIO IS WALKING INTO THE INNER COURTYARD OF AN Italian villa—the frescoed walls with classic Italian art; the smell of crusty bread, fresh spices, and roasting garlic; and the warm embrace and kiss on each cheek by owner Mauro Golmarvi. Mauro's passion and enthusiasm for his food and his patrons is evidenced in the robustness of his welcome and the palate pleasing presentation of his courses.

Beginning with the classic antipasti plate, you're led into the culinary delights of risotto, soups, pasta, and meat dishes. Savor the smell and the flavor of Assaggio's Fusilli Zafferano: sausage, pine nuts, arugula, currants, and saffron cream sauce or Agnello Marchigiana: braised lamb shanks, fresh herbs, and Italian plum tomatoes. Sip on wines from Assaggio's international wine selection from the restaurant's extensive wine cellar, recipient of *Wine Spectator Magazine*'s Award of Excellence.

As your mind and body meld into the atmosphere, the meal, the convivial conversation, the wine, you'll find yourself transported to a simpler time and another place. You'll want to top your lunch or dinner with Assaggio's classic Tiramisu and a cup of espresso. As you leave, you'll feel relaxed and satisfied; pleased to know you've discovered the restaurant personality who is Mauro and a favorite new spot that is Assaggio Ristorante.

4

Gamberoni alla Griglia

SERVES 4

Combine goat cheese, lemon juice, mint, water, and vinegar in saucepan. Stir and cook on medium heat until creamy. In sauté pan, sauté prawns with olive oil and salt and pepper until well done.

Dip prawns in sauce and arrange around salad in middle of plate. Garnish with lemon wedges and serve.

2 TBSP EXTRA VIRGIN OLIVE OIL
1 LB WILD GULF PRAWNS, PEELED AND DEVEINED
20 OZ GOAT CHEESE, CRUMBLED
3 TBSP LEMON JUICE
PINCH MINT
2 TBSP WATER
2 TSP BALSAMIC VINEGAR
2 LEMONS, CUT INTO WEDGES
1 CUP MIXED GREEN SALAD

Insalata di Panzanella

SERVES 4

In aluminum bowl, combine all ingredients. Add extra virgin olive oil and water. Whisk together. Add salt and pepper to taste. Let stand for 20 minutes. Serve and enjoy.

2 LBS DARK BREAD, DICED
6 ROMA TOMATOES, DICED
1 WHOLE RED ONION, DICED
12 SPRIGS BASIL, CHOPPED
12 SPRIGS ITALIAN PARSLEY, CHOPPED
6 CLOVES GARLIC, MINCED
1 CAN CANNELINI BEANS, DRAINED
1 CUP EXTRA VIRGIN OLIVE OIL

5

Linguine alla Mauro

SERVES 4

Cook pasta in boiling water with a dash of salt for 5 minutes while preparing sauce. In sauté pan, sauté garlic and eggplant in olive oil until garlic is golden. Add marinara sauce and wine. Bring to a boil. Add prawns and cream. Stir and reduce to simmer. Drain pasta and add to sauce with basil. Stir and serve. Garnish with parsley.

1 LB LINGUINE
2 LB FRESH PRAWNS
2 TBSP OLIVE OIL
1/2 CUP DRY WHITE WINE
1/4 PINT HEAVY WHIPPING CREAM
1 EGGPLANT, CUBED
1 TBSP GARLIC, CHOPPED
5 OZ MARINARA SAUCE
1 OZ BASIL, CHOPPED
1 OZ ITALIAN PARSLEY, CHOPPED FINE
SALT AND PEPPER TO TASTE

Porchetta
Ripiene al
Portobello

❖ STUFFED PORK

4 PORK CHOPS,
2-3" THICK
4 SLICES PROSCIUTTO,
THINLY SLICED
4 SLICES FONTINA CHEESE,
THINLY SLICED
8 SAGE LEAVES, WHOLE
SALT AND PEPPER TO TASTE

❖ RISOTTO

1 CUP ITALIAN ARBORIO RICE
1/2 CUP ONIONS, DICED 1/4"
2 TBSP BUTTER, UNSALTED
1/2 CUP BAROLO WINE
1 CUP WATER AT A ROLLING BOIL
1/2 CUP VEAL STOCK
SALT AND PEPPER TO TASTE

❖ SAUCE

2 PORTOBELLO MUSHROOMS,
MEDIUM CAPS, STEMMED
AND SLICED 1/4"
2 CLOVES GARLIC, COARSELY CHOPPED
1/8 CUP OLIVE OIL
3/8 CUP BAROLO WINE
1 CUP VEAL STOCK
1-2 TBSP BUTTER, UNSALTED
FLOUR, AS NEEDED
SALT AND PEPPER TO TASTE

SERVES 4

❖ Lay a pork chop flat on a cutting board with the bone facing up and the meat to the right. Make an opening in the side of the chop to the bone. Carefully hollow out the inside to about 1/4" from the edges. Do not pierce the sides. Repeat for the three remaining chops. Stack the prosciutto, fontina and sage leaves together. Fold over once. Stuff each of the chops, making sure the stuffing is spread evenly inside. Brush with olive oil. Season with salt and pepper. When ready to serve, grill the chops until medium to medium well, about 4 to 6 minutes per side. (The time will vary depending on the size of the pork chop.)

❖ In a heavy bottom sauté pan, melt 1 1/2 tbsp butter. Sauté the onions until translucent. Add the rice and sauté, stirring constantly for 3 to 4 minutes. Add the Barolo and half the water. Cook, stirring constantly until all the water is absorbed. Add the rest of the water. Cook, stirring constantly until it is all absorbed. Add the veal stock, salt, pepper, and butter. Simmer until rice is just cooked and has a creamy texture.

❖ In another heavy bottom sauté pan, heat the olive oil with the salt, pepper, and garlic. Cook the garlic until golden brown. Add the portobello mushrooms. Sauté for 1 minute. Add the Barolo wine. Reduce by one half. Add the veal stock. Reduce by two-thirds. Add the butter rolled in the flour. Cook until sauce is fairly thick and shiny.

ASSEMBLY

It is best to have the sauce and risotto almost ready when starting to grill the chops. When the chops are finished, place one fourth of the risotto in the center of each plate. Put a pork chop on each mound of risotto with bone side facing in. Divide the sauce equally among the four plates. If the sauce has become too dry, add water or more veal stock.

The best way to purchase the pork chops is to go to your local butcher and ask for milk fed or free range pork rib chops, frenched, and prepped for stuffing. Don and Joe's Meat in the Pike Place Market is a great place to find excellent quality pork.

Veal stock can be made using traditional recipes, but I recommend buying Demiglace Gold, a product found in higher end grocery stores such as Larry's Markets and Thriftway.

Tiramisu

SERVES 4

1 14 OZ PKG LADYFINGERS
3 CUPS COFFEE
1/2 CUP MARSALA WINE
1 CUP ESPRESSO
1/2 CUP SUGAR
1 QT HEAVY WHIPPING CREAM
4 OZ CREAM CHEESE
4 OZ MASCARPONE
1 CUP SUGAR
4 WHOLE EGGS
COCOA POWDER, AS NEEDED

Combine coffee, marsala, espresso and 1/2 cup sugar for soaking the ladyfingers. Combine whipping cream, cream cheese, mascarpone cheese, 1 cup sugar, and eggs for the cream layer.

Soak each ladyfinger individually in the coffee mixture. Layer in the bottom of a shallow pan. Add a 2" layer of cream mixture. Add another layer of ladyfingers soaked in coffee mixture. Add another 2" layer of cream mixture. Smooth surface. Sprinkle with cocoa powder. Refrigerate 24 hours. Cut and serve.

Wine Pairing

8

GAMBERONI ALLA GRIGLIA
2002 VIERRA CLARET
WALLA WALLA VALLEY

INSALATA DI PANZANELLA
2002 VIERRA SYRAH
WALLA WALLA VALLEY

LINGUINE ALLA MAURO
2001 BASEL CELLARS MERRIMENT
WALLA WALLA VALLEY

PORCHETTA RIPIENE AL PORTOBELLO
2002 BASEL CELLARS SYRAH
COLUMBIA VALLEY

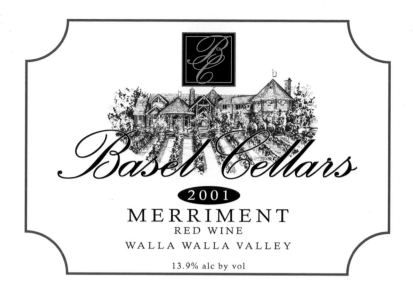

2001

MERRIMENT
RED WINE
WALLA WALLA VALLEY

13.9% alc by vol

BASEL CELLARS

GREG AND BECKY BASEL,
STEVE AND JO MARIE HANSEN,
OWNERS

2901 OLD MILTON HIGHWAY
WALLA WALLA, WA 99362
509.522.0200
www.baselcellars.com

OUR WINEMAKING PHILOSOPHY IS SIMPLE...GENTLE AND MINIMAL HANDLING at each step in the winemaking process. We pick fruit at its optimal maturity level to express the true flavors of the grape and the site. After strict taste trials, only the very best barrels, from the very best lots, will go into the Basel Cellars portfolio. The rest of the wines will be crafted into the Vierra Vineyards wines.

Basel Cellars Estate Winery is in the heart of Washington's Walla Walla Valley. The winery is the perfect place to stage every celebration of life—reunions with family and friends, invigorating romantic escapes, memorable weddings—and the ideal venue for an executive retreat or casual corporate meeting. The grounds, the Resort, the facilities are one-of-a-kind. The main building design invokes the spirit of casual grandeur found in venerable American lodges such as Yosemite's Awahnee Lodge and Mt. Hood's Timberline Lodge. The eclectic combination of handcrafted woodwork, natural stone masonry, an abundance of windows, and incomparable comfort celebrate the style and character of the Pacific Northwest.

The Estate features luxury overnight accommodations for up to eighteen guests in the rustic yet elegant 13,000 square foot facility, complete with gated security, comfortable meeting rooms, gourmet kitchen, fireplaces, hottubs, sauna, theater, theme bar, private outdoor pool, and separate poolside cabaña. Basel Cellars offers acres of landscaped gardens, patios and vineyards overlooking the Walla Walla River with vistas of wheat covered foothills nestled against regal violet mountain silhouettes.

We set a new standard for the Northwest-style "getaway" experience.

Salmon Trio: House Cured Gravlax, Alder Smoked Salmon Mousse, and Salmon Caviar with

Horseradish Crème and Toasted Rye

Chopped Endive Salad with Roasted Apples, Roquefort Cheese, Hazelnut Pralines,

and Citrus Vinaigrette

Maple Cured Pork Loin Chop with Twice Baked Yukon Potato, Sautéed Spinach and Pear–thyme Coulis

Cookie Crusted Coconut Cheesecake with Chocolate–Passion Fruit Glaze

Brasserie Margaux

BRASSERIE MARGAUX
IN THE WARWICK HOTEL
CHRIS ZARKADES,
EXECUTIVE CHEF

401 LENORA STREET
SEATTLE, WA 98121
206.777.1990
www.margauxseattle.com

THE CHARM AND APPEAL OF BRASSERIE MARGAUX IS NOT JUST CONFINED to its handsome dark wood, beautifully muraled ceiling, or cozy bar. Executive Chef Chris Zarkades has crafted an enticing seasonal menu that expertly integrates continental offerings with creative Northwest cuisine. There are items that are direct descendants of the French brasserie, such as Brasserie Margaux's traditional (and incomparable) French onion soup. There is a bow to Spanish fare, such as the restaurant's Paella and the bar's Tapas menu. And there are Chef Zarkades' unique Northwest creations, including his fantastic Dungeness crab cakes (considered one of the best in Seattle). Among the not-to-be missed desserts is the restaurant's signature Chocolate Banana Torte, as well as the nightly offerings of two different flavors of crème brulée.

The by-the-glass wine selection is very reasonably priced, and the wine list is a nice combination of Northwest and European wines. (The list naturally includes a 1978 Chateau Margaux!) Brasserie Margaux offers monthly prix-fixe wine dinners that showcase both Chef Zarkades' efforts and the wines of a single vintner, such as McCrea Cellars.

Brasserie Margaux has received *Wine Spectator*'s Award of Excellence, and was recently named one of Seattle's best brunches by AOL Cityguide. (The restaurant offers breakfast, lunch, and dinner, and year 'round three course prix-fixe lunch and dinner specials at very reasonable prices). Brasserie Margaux is part of the Warwick Hotel in downtown Seattle. Its entrance is directly across from the Cinerama Theater, which makes Brasserie Margaux the ideal pre- or post-theater gathering place.

*Salmon Trio: House Cured Gravlax,
Alder Smoked Salmon Mousse, and Salmon Caviar with
Horseradish Crème and Toasted Rye*

12 COLD SMOKED SALMON LOX
2 OZ CAPERS
1 TBSP CHIVES, CHOPPED
1 LEMON
6 SLICES QUALITY RYE BREAD
1/4 CUP CHOPPED CHIVES
1 OZ OLIVE OIL
1 1/2 OZ SEASONAL MIXED GREENS
SALT AND WHITE PEPPER

❖ ALDER SMOKED MOUSSE
4 OZ ALDER SMOKED SALMON,
SKIN AND PELLICLE REMOVED
1 OZ CREAM CHEESE
4 OZ HEAVY WHIPPING CREAM

❖ HORSERADISH CREAM SAUCE
1 TSP PREPARED HORSERADISH
8 OZ CRÈME FRAÎCHE
(SUBSTITUTE SOUR CREAM)
1 TBSP LEMON JUICE
PINCH OF SALT
WHITE PEPPER TO TASTE

SERVES 6

This can be prepared up to a day in advance.

❖ In a food processor with blade attachment, purée the alder smoked salmon, cream cheese and 1 oz of the cream until mixture is very smooth. Scrape down sides of the processor to ensure all is puréed. Transfer to a small mixing bowl.

In another small mixing bowl with a whip, beat the remaining cream to a soft peak. Transfer half of the whipped cream to the bowl with the salmon paste. Mix in to lighten the paste. Gently fold in the remaining cream with a rubber spatula just until mixed. Be sure not to overmix. Refrigerate until needed.

❖ In a small bowl, whisk together crème fraîche, horseradish, 1 tbsp lemon juice, a pinch of salt, and white pepper to taste. Refrigerate until needed.

ASSEMBLY

Dress the greens in a bowl with olive oil and lemon juice. Arrange a small nest of greens in the center of each plate. Divide lox slices by 6 and roll up the slices lengthwise to form a rose or circle leaving a 1 1/2" void in the center. Place lox rose atop the greens. Fill the void with a dollop of the salmon mousse. Top the mousse with a spoonful of caviar. Drizzle sauce around greens. Sprinkle the whole plate with the capers and chives. Toast rye bread and cut each slice into 4 triangle points. Place rye toast points around the edge of the plate. Serve immediately.

Endive Salad with Roasted Apples and Hazelnut Pralines

SERVES 6

❖ In a small saucepan over medium to high heat, reduce by one-half its volume—orange juice, rice wine vinegar, and sliced shallots. Let cool. Transfer to a blender and purée while slowly adding salad oil. Season with salt and pepper.

❖ Cut the apple quarters in half. Heat a large enough skillet to cook the apples in one layer. Add butter and brown sugar. Stir to form a simple caramel. Carefully place apples into pan and stir to coat while searing the apple. Deglaze with brandy when apples are tender and caramelized. Remove from pan and spread out on a sheet pan. Keep warm.

❖ Place the warm apple wedges at 3 points on the plate. Toss the endive, greens, cheese, and half the nuts with the dressing. Arrange between the 6 plates in the center of the plate. Sprinkle with nuts and drizzle extra vinaigrette around the edge of the plate.

❖ VINAIGRETTE
8 OZ ORANGE JUICE
2 OZ RICE WINE VINEGAR
1/2 OZ SHALLOTS, SLICED
6 OZ OF SALAD OIL
SALT AND PEPPER

❖ APPLES
3 RED DELICIOUS APPLES, CORED AND QUARTERED
2 OZ WHOLE BUTTER
3 OZ BROWN SUGAR
2 OZ BRANDY (OPTIONAL)

❖ GREENS
5 TO 6 HEADS BELGIAN ENDIVE, CUT INTO 1/2" PIECES
2 OZ SEASONAL SALAD GREENS, CUT INTO 1/2" PIECES
6 OZ ROQUEFORT CHEESE, CRUMBLED
2 OZ CANDIED HAZELNUTS, CRUSHED (OR SUBSTITUTE WITH ANY TYPE OF PRALINE)
6 TO 7 OZ VINAIGRETTE
18 CARAMELIZED APPLE WEDGES

13

Maple Cured Pork Loin Chop, Twice-Baked Yukon Potato, Sautéed Spinach, and Pear-Thyme Coulis

❖ MAPLE BRINE

2 CUPS WATER
.8 OZ SALT
4 OZ BROWN SUGAR
3/4 OZ MAPLE EXTRACT
1/2 MEDIUM ONION, SLICED
4 TSP BLACK PEPPER
2 SPRIGS THYME
2 SPRIGS ROSEMARY
2 OZ BRANDY
4 BAY LEAVES
1/2 OZ GARLIC, CHOPPED
6 - 10 OZ PORK CHOPS,
1 1/4" THICK

❖ TWICE-BAKED YUKON POTATO

6 MEDIUM SIZE YUKON POTATOES
3 OZ WHOLE BUTTER, SOFTENED
1 1/2 OZ GRUYERE CHEESE, GRATED
2 TBSP CHIVES, CHOPPED
SALT AND PEPPER

❖ PEAR-THYME COULIS

3 PEARS, PEELED, CORED
AND 1/2" DICED
1/2 CUP ONION, DICED
1 TSP GINGER, CHOPPED
1 TBSP FRESH THYME, CHOPPED
1/2 CUP SUGAR
1 CUP WHITE WINE
JUICE OF 1 LIME
ZEST OF 1 LIME

❖ SAUTÉED SPINACH

1 1/2 OZ OLIVE OIL
1 OZ SHALLOTS
1 LB SPINACH LEAVES
1 OZ WHITE WINE
1 LEMON

SERVES 6

❖ Bring all ingredients except for the pork chops to boil in a 2 quart saucepan. Remove from heat. Let cool to room temperature. Place pork chops and the brine in a small container so that the chops are completely covered. Refrigerate for 20 to 24 hours. Remove chops from the brine. Lightly rinse with fresh water and pat with paper towel. Reserve for cooking.

Potatoes can be prepared in advance and refrigerated until needed.

❖ Bake potatoes in 400° oven until tender, 45 minutes to 1 hour, depending on size. When cooled enough to handle, yet still warm, slice 1/4" off the bottom to allow potato to stand on end. Slice off top 1/3 of potato. With small spoon, scoop out the center without damaging the shell. Place scooped out potato into a bowl and mash with the butter, cheese, chives, and salt and pepper to taste. Refill potato shells with mixture. To reheat, bake at 375° for 20 to 30 minutes, depending on size.

❖ Place all ingredients in a 2 quart saucepan over medium heat. Stew until tender, about 1 1/2 hours. Remove from heat and let cool. Purée in a blender or food processor until smooth.

❖ Heat a large pot. Add olive oil and sliced shallots to the pot and sweat until soft. Pack spinach into the pot. Sprinkle with 1 oz white wine and the juice of 1/2 lemon. With tongs, turn spinach, and allow to wilt until tender. Season with salt and pepper.

Preheat oven to 375°. Place potatoes in oven on a greased baking sheet. Sprinkle chops with black pepper. Heat an ovenproof skillet on medium to high heat. Add 1 oz olive oil and sear chops on 1 side. Invert chops and place into oven to pan roast until medium—150° in the center. This should take 18 to 20 minutes, depending on thickness of the pork chops.

Remove pork and potatoes when done and let rest for 10 minutes. Meanwhile, heat pear coulis, and sauté spinach. Arrange spinach on the center of the plate with potato next to it. Place pork chop atop the spinach. Coat with coulis. Serve.

14

Coconut Cheesecake with Chocolate-Passion Fruit Glaze

SERVES 12-14

✤ Preheat oven to 350°. In the bowl of a food processor, process first 3 ingredients until nuts are chopped fine. Slowly drizzle in melted butter until mixture comes together. Press into the bottom of a 9" cake pan. Bake for 10 minutes or until coconut and nuts are toasted golden brown. Transfer to a wire rack to cool.

✤ Preheat oven to 300°. In the bowl of an electric mixer fitted with a paddle attachment, combine the cream cheese with the sugar. Beat on low speed until smooth and creamy, scraping down the bowl and paddle with a rubber spatula as necessary. Slowly add the vanilla extract and the coconut milk. Scrape down the bowl thoroughly. Mix in eggs, one at a time.

Pour the cheesecake batter into the prepared pan and set in a large baking dish or roasting pan. Place in the middle of the oven. Pour enough very hot water into the pan to come 3/4 of the way up the cake pan. Bake for 70 minutes until edges are firm and center jiggles slightly.

Remove cheesecake from the water and cool for 1 hour. Refrigerate for at least 4 hours or overnight. To remove from pan, run a thin-bladed knife around the outer edge of the cheese-cake. Set pan directly over low heat for a few seconds, turn onto plate, then invert onto serving plate.

✤ Finely chop the chocolate and place in a mixing bowl. In a small saucepan, boil the cream with the passion fruit purée and sugar. Pour over the chocolate and whisk together. While still very warm, pour over the top of the cheesecake, spreading glaze to the edges. Press coconut into the sides of the cheesecake. Garnish with macadamia nuts and toasted coconut.

✤ CRUST

1/2 CUP CHOCOLATE COOKIE CRUMBS
1/4 CUP MACADAMIA NUTS
1/2 CUP COCONUT, SHREDDED
1 TBSP BUTTER, MELTED

✤ CHEESECAKE FILLING

2 LB CREAM CHEESE, SOFTENED
1 CUP COCONUT PURÉE
5 EGGS, ROOM TEMPERATURE
1 TBSP VANILLA EXTRACT
1 1/2 CUPS SUGAR
1 CUP COCONUT, SHREDDED

✤ CHOCOLATE AND PASSION FRUIT GLAZE

3 TBSP CREAM
4 OZ SEMI SWEET CHOCOLATE
3 TBSP PASSION FRUIT PURÉE
1 TBSP SUGAR

15

Wine Pairing

16

SALMON TRIO: HOUSE CURED GRAVLAX, ALDER SMOKED SALMON MOUSSE,
AND SALMON CAVIAR WITH HORSERADISH CRÈME AND TOASTED RYE
2003 VIN ROSÉ
WASHINGTON STATE

CHOPPED ENDIVE SALAD WITH ROASTED APPLES, ROQUEFORT CHEESE,
HAZELNUT PRALINES, AND CITRUS VINAIGRETTE
2003 ROUSSANNE
RED MOUNTAIN

MAPLE CURED PORK LOIN CHOP WITH TWICE BAKED YUKON POTATO,
SAUTÉED SPINACH AND PEAR–THYME COULIS
2002 SIROCCO
WASHINGTON STATE
(GRENACHE, SYRAH, MOURVÈDRE, COUNOISE)

COOKIE CRUSTED COCONUT CHEESECAKE WITH CHOCOLATE,
PASSION FRUIT GLAZE
2002 LATE HARVEST VIOGNIER
WASHINGTON STATE

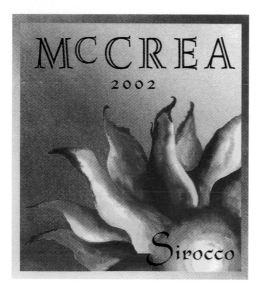

MCCREA
2002

Sirocco

OWNED AND OPERATED BY TWO COUPLES—DOUG AND KIM MCCREA (AND their sons Kevin and Kalen) and Bob and Susan Neel (and their four cats)— McCrea Cellars is Washington's first winery dedicated to Rhône varietals. Winemaker and 'Rhône Ranger', Doug McCrea, transforms grapes from Washington's finest vineyards into wines of extraordinary depth, balance, complexity, and finesse.

McCrea's first Rhône grapes came from gnarled mature Grenache vines growing in the Columbia River Gorge. In the early 1990s, McCrea made a popular red Rhône blend of Syrah and Grenache called Tierra del Sol. The Cellar's first varietal Syrah came from the 1994 vintage. McCrea's 1997 Viognier was the first Viognier ever released in Washington State. McCrea now has six Rhône varietals in the winery— Syrah, Grenache, Mourvèdre, Counoise, Viognier and Roussanne. Marsanne will be harvested with the 2004 vintage and Cinsault, Picpoul, and Grenache Blanc will be planted this year.

Pioneering Rhône grapes in Washington has required patience and careful selection of vineyard sites. Eastern Washington's fine soils, unique latitude, and desert climate are now recognized as ideal for turning out Rhône wines of great fruit intensity, structure, and complexity. Annually producing 3400 cases, McCrea Cellars is proud to be at the forefront of the Northwest's rapidly expanding Rhône-wine offerings.

MCCREA
CELLARS

DOUG AND KIM MCCREA,
SUSAN AND BOB NEEL,
OWNERS

7533 34TH AVENUE SW

SEATTLE, WA 98126

206.938.8643

www.mccreacellars.com

GAMBAS AL AJILLO

CEVICHE TOSTADAS

SEARED PORK ADOBO

MOLTEN LAVA CAKE

Cactus

CACTUS

4220 E MADISON

SEATTLE, WA 98112

206.324.4140

121 PARK LANE

KIRKLAND, WA 98033

425.893.9799

www.cactusrestaurants.com

COMBINE THE BRIGHT COLORS OF A FRIDA KAHLO PAINTING, RELIABLY spectacular Southwestern and Mexican food, and a playful, festive atmosphere, and you have Cactus. Cactus in Seattle's Madison Park neighborhood is as close to New Mexico as you'll get in the Northwest unless you decide to drive across Lake Washington to visit the second Cactus in Kirkland! The restaurants have identical menus, and both draw eager crowds and collect uniformly outstanding reviews.

The menu at Cactus is well-chosen and imaginative. A substantial part of the menu is devoted to tapas offerings, including artichoke quesadillas, ceviche tostadas, coconut prawns, and grilled asparagus adorned with a fantastic chipotle sauce. The entrée menu includes Cactus' flawless updates of delicious standards, such as fajitas, fish tacos, and pork steak adobo—seared pork tenderloin with citrus adobo, coconut lime rice, achiote black beans, and smoked Fresno chile pineapple salsa. Cactus also offers daily originals including mojito marinated Alaskan halibut wrapped in a banana leaf with mango mint salsa and pineapple ginger rice and slow-roasted pork carnitas tamales with jack cheese. Save room for the Cuban flan, which is a touch of heaven here on earth.

Cactus makes the best handmade margaritas around, serving sixteen different tequilas. Its Cuban mojitos—made from rum, mint, and lime juice—are a great complement to the flavorful food. When the weather gods are kind, an outdoor table at either restaurant is a delightful place to spend an evening.

Gambas al Ajillo

2 CUP OLIVE OIL

1 CUP GARLIC CLOVES,
PEELED AND ROUGH CHOPPED

7 CHILE DE ARBOL

9 SPRIGS THYME

3 SPRIGS ROSEMARY

2 TSP SALT

1 TSP BLACK PEPPER

1/4 CUP DRY SHERRY

1 LEMON, CUT IN QUARTERS

28 PRAWNS, PEELED
AND DE-VEINED BUT WITH
THE TAIL LEFT ON
(FOR APPEARANCE)

SERVES 4

In a large sauté pan, place all ingredients except sherry, lemon and prawns. Turn heat on medium high. When garlic starts to turn golden, add prawns. When prawns turn orangish, turn heat all the way up. Add dry sherry. (If you are making this on an electric stove, you will have to light the pan with a match or lighter to burn off the alcohol.)

Squeeze juice from all 4 quarters of lemon into the pan and add lemon pieces as well. Place in dishes for your guests or toothpick them and serve as appetizers.

If you are serving them in meal portions, we suggest serving bread with them. This is a good dish to mop up because the oil has plenty of flavor.

caramelize lightly. Transfer mushrooms to an appropriate size strainer to drain away excess butter. Repeat for each mushroom variety. Save butter.

✤ Take equal parts mushroom scraps and a mirepoix of carrots, onions, and leeks and process to fine in a food processor. In a stockpot, sauté this mixture until aromatic. Add bay leaves, black peppercorns, mustard seeds, parsley stems, and thyme sprigs. Cover with water. Bring to a boil.

Reduce to a simmer and cook until a nice mushroom flavor is achieved. Strain. Reserve stock. Return vegetables to pot and cover with fresh water. Simmer again. Strain. Combine both stocks and reduce to rich mushroom taste.

✤ MUSHROOM STOCK

MUSHROOM SCRAPS
MIREPOIX (A SAUTÉED MIXTURE
OF VEGETABLES USED TO FLAVOR
STOCKS AND SOUPS)
1/3 CARROTS
1/3 ONIONS
1/3 LEEKS
2-3 TBSP OLIVE OIL
1 BAY LEAF
1/2 TSP FRESH CRACKED
BLACK PEPPERCORNS
1/2 TSP MUSTARD SEEDS
3 PARSLEY STEMS
1 THYME SPRIG

29

ASSEMBLY

✤ In a medium sauté pan on medium heat, add 3 tbsp of the reserved mushroom butter. Add sautéed mushrooms. Heat through, tossing regularly. Add shallots and brown lightly. Drain excess butter. Return to heat. Add Cognac, flame, then add white wine (turn off your gas flame when adding wine or any other alcohol). Heat until reduced to dry. Add mushroom stock. Reduce to almost dry. Add thyme. Adjust seasoning with salt and fresh ground pepper.

On a heated plate (heated in oven for 30 seconds to 1 minute) add 1 tbsp grated Parmesan. Place mushroom in center in a little stack. Top with shaved Parmesan sheets.

✤ ASSEMBLY

PREPARED MUSHROOMS
3 TBSP RESERVED
MUSHROOM BUTTER
2 TBSP SHALLOTS, MINCED
1/2 CUP DRY WHITE WINE
1-2 OZ COGNAC OR BRANDY
1/2 CUP MUSHROOM STOCK
1 TSP THYME
SEA SALT AND FRESH GROUND
PEPPER TO TASTE
4 TO 8 TBSP PARMESAN, GRATED
4 1"X 2" PARMESAN SHEETS,
CUT WITH A VEGETABLE PEELER

Tartare de Boeuf aux Herbes

12 OZ RIBEYE, PARTIALLY FROZEN,
FREE OF FAT OR SILVER SKIN

1 TSP CAPERS, DRAINED AND CHOPPED

1 TBSP SHALLOTS, MINCED

2 TSP DIJON MUSTARD

1 TBSP PARSLEY, CHOPPED

2-3 TSP EXTRA VIRGIN OLIVE OIL

1/2 TSP LEMON JUICE

SEL GRIS (FRENCH GREY SEA SALT)
TO TASTE

FRESH GROUND BLACK PEPPER TO TASTE

2 BELGIAN ENDIVE, JULIENNE

4 OZ DAIKON RADISH, JULIENNE

8 3/4" SLICES PAN DE MIE

❖ CREAMY MUSTARD
VINAIGRETTE

MAKES 1 CUP, USE THE REST AS
A SALAD DRESSING

2 EGG YOLKS

1 TBSP DIJON MUSTARD

2 TSP SHALLOTS, MINCED FINE

1 1/2 OZ RICE VINEGAR

3/4 CUP OLIVE OIL OR GRAPESEED OIL

SEA SALT TO TASTE

FRESH GROUND BLACK PEPPER TO TASTE

❖ SAUCE

4 EGG YOLKS

4 TBSP CREAMY MUSTARD VINAIGRETTE

1 TBSP PARSLEY, CHOPPED

1 TSP PARSLEY PURÉE (OPTIONAL)

SERVES 4

Wrap beef in plastic wrap and place in the freezer. This will make cutting much easier.

Dice beef into 3/8" cubes. Combine diced beef with capers, shallots, Dijon mustard, parsley, extra virgin olive oil, and lemon juice. Mix thoroughly but gently with a spoon. Avoid smashing beef. Adjust seasoning with salt and pepper. Shape into a patty or quenelles (egg shape made with two spoons). Toast pan de mie to a nice golden brown.

❖ In a 1 quart non-reactive bowl, whisk together egg yolks, mustard, shallots, and vinegar.

Slowly drizzle oil until a nice emulsion is formed. Adjust to taste with sea salt and fresh ground pepper.

❖ Combine egg yolks, vinaigrette, and chopped parsley. Toss with julienne endive and radish. Adjust seasoning with salt and pepper and lemon juice (if needed).

PARSLEY PURÉE

This produces the bright green color of the sauce. Blanch parsley in hot water. Cool in an ice bath. Blend into a smooth purée. Pass through a tamis (French drum sieve).

If there is sauce left over, drizzle on the plate.

Twice Baked Chocolate Gâteau

SERVES 4

3 OZ HIGH QUALITY BITTERSWEET
CHOCOLATE
6 TBSP BUTTER
1/4 CUP PLUS 1 TSP COCOA POWDER,
ALKALIZED OR DUTCHED, EUROPEAN
STYLE
2 EXTRA LARGE EGGS, SEPARATED
1/2 CUP PLUS 2 TBSP SUGAR, DIVIDED IN
2 PORTIONS

Preheat oven to 325°.

Chop chocolate. Put in a bowl with the butter and cocoa powder. Place the bowl over a pot of boiling water. Turn off heat. Let everything melt, stirring occasionally.

Prepare a sheet pan lined with parchment paper and 4 3" rings sprayed with non-stick cooking spray. Whip yolks with one portion of sugar at high speed until very light in color and thick (2 to 3 minutes or longer by hand). Whip whites, adding the rest of the sugar gradually, until glossy and forming stiff peaks. With a rubber spatula, fold the egg yolk mixture into slightly warm chocolate mixture. Add the egg white mixture, fold in as well. Fill the rings 2/3 full. Reserve remaining batter.

Bake for 15 to 20 minutes or until the top is set and somewhat firm to the touch but the inside is still very soft. Let cool. Divide the remaining batter between the 4 gâteaux by carefully spooning it on top of the cakes. Chill.

20 minutes before serving, bake the gâteaux again for 15 minutes at 400°. Let set for a few minutes. Remove the rings. Serve with your favorite ice cream.

31

Wine Pairing

LEEKS IN TRUFFLE VINAIGRETTE
GRENACHE ROSÉ
COLUMBIA VALLEY

CHAMPIGNONS SAUVAGES WITH PARMESAN
VIOGNIER
CLIFTON VINEYARD

TARTARE DE BOEUF AUX HERBES
ROUSSANNE
ALDER RIDGE VINEYARD

TWICE BAKED CHOCOLATE GÂTEAU
RESERVE SYRAH
COLUMBIA VALLEY

32

Syncline
wine cellars

Syrah

2002
Columbia Valley
Milbrandt Vineyards

SYNCLINE
WINE CELLARS

JAMES AND POPPIE MANTONE,
OWNERS

307 W HUMBOLDT STREET

BINGEN, WA 98605

509.365.4361

www.synclinewine.com

SYNCLINE WINE CELLARS WAS STARTED IN 1999 BY JAMES AND POPPIE Mantone, with the intention of exploring the potential of Rhône varietals in Washington State. We are dedicated to producing Washington State wines of unique personality and distinction. Grapes are sourced throughout the Columbia Valley, from the alluvial soils of the Wahluke Slope to the ancient volcanic soils of the Horse Heaven Hills. Distinctive vineyard sites matched with dedicated winemaking yield wines of incredible richness, structure, and intensity.

A line up of single vineyard Syrah is complimented by Grenache, Viognier, and Roussanne. Cuvée Elena, named after our daughter, is a special reserve blend of Grenache, Syrah, and Mourvedre modeled after the great wines of Chateuneuf du Pape. To ensure the fine quality, yearly production is limited to no more than 2500 cases. Located in the Columbia River Gorge, we offer a quick escape to the incomparable beauty of Washington's wine country.

AGEDASHI TOFU

KABOCHA, SWEET ONION, AND SPINACH MISO

BARA CHIRASHI

SATSUMA YAM PIE

Chiso

CHISO RESTAURANT
TAICHI KITAMURA, OWNER
AND EXECUTIVE CHEF

3520 FREMONT AVENUE N

SEATTLE, WA 98103

206.632.3430

www.chisoseattle.com

CHISO RESTAURANT WILL DELIGHT YOU WITH THE NORTHWEST'S MOST sublime Japanese cuisine. Using only the freshest seafood and ingredients, Owner and Executive Chef Taichi Kitamura creates high quality sushi, hand picked seasonal specialties, and unique appetizers. Chiso's menu items are as pleasing to your eye as they are delectable to your palate. Catering to even the most refined tastes, we offer traditional Japanese fare, regional favorites, and vegetarian dishes. We also serve an unusual and exquisite cuisine for those with an adventurous appetite.

Located in the heart of Fremont, our culinary delights are presented to you in a casually elegant, soothing, Zen-like ambiance.

Agedashi Tofu

1 LB BLOCK OF MEDIUM FIRM TOFU
PAPER TOWELS

SAUCE
1 1/4 CUPS WATER
1/4 CUP MIRIN* (SWEET RICE WINE)
1/4 CUP SOY SAUCE
1 1/2 TSP DASHI POWDER*

GARNISHES
1-2 STALKS OF GREEN ONION
1/4-1/2 PIECE OF DAIKON*
(JAPANESE RADISH)
1 PIECE OF FRESH GINGER ROOT
DRIED BONITO FLAKES*

BOWL OF CORNSTARCH
FOR COATING TOFU
VEGETABLE OIL FOR DEEP FRYING

SERVES 4

Drain the tofu and cut it into sixteen pieces (see diagram below). Gently pat dry with a paper towel.

Side View   Top View

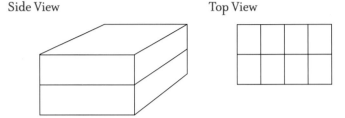

To prepare the sauce, place all ingredients in a pot and bring to a boil. Set aside.

Peel ginger and daikon. Using a fine grater (oroshigane—metal Japanese grater), grate the ginger and daikon separately. Drain each in a sieve. To make the garnish, take about 1/2 to 1 teaspoon of grated daikon and gently squeeze out the excess water. Shape into a pyramid and place a small pinch of grated ginger on top. Repeat for the other 3 servings. Set aside.

Slice the green onions into thin rings, about 1 to 2 tablespoons. Set aside.

Preheat the oil to 350° in a deep fryer or wok. Or to fry in a skillet, add about 1" of oil and heat to 350°. Evenly coat tofu by rolling in cornstarch. Fry until golden brown. If using a skillet, you will need to turn the tofu over until it is golden brown on all sides. Place on rack or towels to drain.

For one serving (4 pieces), arrange the fried tofu in the bowl and place the daikon-ginger garnish on top of one of the pieces. To finish, sprinkle green onions, a generous pinch of bonito flakes, and add sauce until it covers about 2/3 of the bottom pieces.

36

Kabocha, Sweet Onion, and Spinach Miso

SERVES 4

Place water and dashi powder in a soup pot and bring the water to a boil. After the water comes to a boil, whisk in 5 tablespoons of miso paste. Taste the soup and add more miso paste, if desired. Lower the heat to medium high. Add kabocha and sweet onion. Simmer the soup for 5 to 10 minutes or until the kabocha is soft.

To serve, ladle soup into bowls and evenly divide the spinach for garnish.

❖ Gently wipe the konbu with a dry cloth, taking care not to wipe off the white powdery substance which adds its distinct flavor. Pour the water into a soup pot and soak the konbu for 1 hour.

Place the pot on the stove over medium heat and take out the konbu just before it boils. Add the dried bonito flakes and bring the water to a boil. Do not stir the stock. After the stock comes to a boil, turn off the heat and allow all the flakes to settle to the bottom of the pan. Strain the stock through cheesecloth or a fine mesh strainer. The stock is ready for use.

4 CUPS WATER
1 TBSP DASHI POWDER*
note: to make dashi stock from scratch, see recipe below
5-6 TBSP WHITE MISO PASTE* (ADJUST TO TASTE)
1/2 KABOCHA* (JAPANESE SQUASH), CUT INTO 1" PIECES (APPROXIMATELY 10 OZ)
1/2 SMALL SWEET ONION, CUT INTO THIN STRIPS
4 OZ SPINACH, BLANCHED (PLACED IN BOILING WATER FOR 15 TO 20 SECONDS OR UNTIL WILTED, SUBMERGE IN ICE WATER AND DRAIN). SQUEEZE OUT EXCESS WATER.

❖ DASHI STOCK
4 CUPS WATER
4" LONG PIECE OF KONBU* (DRIED KELP)
1 CUP (10-20 G) DRIED BONITO FLAKES*

37

Bara Chirashi

RICE ✤
2 CUPS SHORT GRAIN RICE
2 1/2 CUPS WATER

SUSHI VINEGAR ✤
1 TBSP SALT
1/4 CUP SUGAR
1/2 CUP + 1 TBSP RICE VINEGAR

SUSHI RICE ✤
COOKED RICE (SEE ABOVE)
3 FL OZ SUSHI VINEGAR (SEE ABOVE)
MEDIUM SHALLOW BOWL OR PLATTER
RICE PADDLE

WASABI SOY SAUCE ✤
1/2 CUP SOY SAUCE
1-2 TBSP WASABI*
NOTE: FOR THIS RECIPE, POWDERED
WASABI IS USED.

SERVES 4

✤ Wash rice by placing in a bowl and covering with cold water. Rub and stir rice vigorously, then drain. Repeat this process of adding water and rubbing the grains of rice until the water is clear, about 2 to 3 times.

Place washed rice in a sieve to drain. Let the rice stand for 30 minutes. Place the rice and water in a heavy pot, cover with a tight fitting lid, and heat the pot on medium heat for 10 minutes. Do not lift the lid during the cooking process. When the water comes to a boil, turn the heat to high for 1 to 2 minutes, then down to low for 15 minutes. Turn the heat to high for 30 seconds and remove from the stove. *Note: An electric rice cooker may be used. Follow the manufacturer's directions.*

Let the rice stand for 10 minutes. Then gently stir the rice.

✤ Combine ingredients in a pot over medium heat. Stir the mixture to dissolve the sugar and salt. Bring the mixture to a boil. Let it cool to room temperature and transfer to a container until ready to use.

✤ *Sushi rice must be made as soon as the rice finishes cooking.*
Transfer the rice into a large shallow bowl. Spread the rice out evenly in the bowl. Hold the rice paddle over the rice and, moving around the surface of the rice, pour the vinegar onto the paddle, so that the vinegar is evenly distributed. Mix the rice with the paddle to incorporate the vinegar.

Let the rice cool to room temperature. Transfer the rice to covered containers, but do not refrigerate. Once the rice is refrigerated, it can no longer be used.

✤ Take 1 tablespoon of wasabi powder and gradually add an approximately equal amount of hot water until it forms a paste. Place in a covered container or turn bowl upside down until ready to use. Place soy sauce in a container with a cover. Add wasabi to the soy sauce and shake until dissolved. Refrigerate until ready to use.

ASSEMBLING THE BARA CHIRASHI

For one serving, place 4 oz of fish in a small bowl. Pour 1 oz wasabi soy sauce on top of the fish. Repeat for remaining three servings. Set aside.

Fill a large bowl with sushi rice no more than half way up the bowl. Do not pack the rice in the bowl. On the surface of the rice, sprinkle sesame seeds and spread 1/2 oz of ginger. Place kizami nori on top of the rice. Mound the fish in the center of the bowl and pour excess sauce around the fish. Garnish with cucumber pieces on top the fish. Sprinkle the kaiware sprouts along the inside edge of the bowl. Finish with a dollop of tobiko on top of the fish. Repeat for remaining three servings.

FOR ASSEMBLY

SUSHI RICE (SEE RECIPE FACING PAGE)
1 LB SUSHI GRADE FISH, CUT INTO 1"
CUBES (4 OZ PER PERSON)
(CHISO'S BARA CHIRASHI CONTAINS
SALMON, YELLOWTAIL, AND TUNA)
TOASTED SESAME SEEDS
2 OZ PICKLED GINGER*, CHOPPED
KIZAMI NORI* (THINLY SLICED NORI)
WASABI SOY SAUCE

GARNISHES

1 CUCUMBER, CUT INTO 1/2" CUBES
KAIWARE* (DAIKON SPROUTS), WASHED
WITH ROOTS CUT OFF (OPTIONAL)
TOBIKO* (OPTIONAL)

Satsuma Yam Pie

YIELDS 2 PIES

✤ Place flour, salt, and sugar into a round-bottomed bowl. Rub the cubed butter into the flour, using fingertips or a pastry cutter, until the mixture resembles fine breadcrumbs. Make a well in the center. Mix the water and lemon zest. Pour into the well of the flour. Mix to form a soft dough. Turn dough out onto a lightly floured work surface. Knead gently just until it is smooth and well mixed. Divide the dough into 2 portions. Wrap in plastic wrap and refrigerate for at least 30 minutes before use.

For each crust, prick the bottom with a fork and prebake at 350° for 10 minutes.

✤ To make the filling, preheat the oven to 450°. Prick yams with a fork. Bake for about 1 to 1 1/2 hours or until skewer comes out clean.

Split the yam in half lengthwise and scrape out the center into a food processor fitted with the metal blade. Add eggs, sugar, mirin, and cream. Process the mixture until smooth. Pour mixture into prebaked pie crusts and bake at 350° until a toothpick inserted in the center comes out clean, about 35 minutes.

Available at Japanese or Asian markets

CRUST

1 RECIPE PÂTÉ BRISÉE OR
2 FROZEN PIE CRUSTS

✤ PÂTÉ BRISÉE

3 3/4 CUPS ALL PURPOSE
OR BREAD FLOUR
1 1/2 TSP KOSHER SALT
1 1/2 TSP SUGAR
1 1/2 CUPS BUTTER, CUT INTO
SMALL CUBES AND CHILLED
1/2 CUP WATER
1/2-1 TSP LEMON ZEST (OPTIONAL)
2 9" PIE PANS
FLOUR FOR ROLLING OUT DOUGH

✤ FILLING

2 LARGE SATSUMA YAMS*
(ABOUT 1 1/2 POUNDS)
3 EGGS
1/2 CUP SUGAR
3 TBSP MIRIN*
1 CUP CREAM

39

Wine Pairing

Agedashi Tofu
2003 San Juan Vineyards Siegerrebe

Kabocha, Sweet Onion, and Spinach Miso
2001 San Juan Vineyards Syrah

Bara Chirashi
2003 San Juan Vineyards Pinot Gris

Satsuma Yam Pie
2001 San Juan Vineyards Gewurztraminer

40

2003 Siegerrebe
Puget Sound

SAN JUAN
VINEYARDS

YVONNE SWANBERG,
OWNER
KURT NIZNIK,
WINEMAKER

3136 ROCHE HARBOR ROAD
FRIDAY HARBOR, WA 98250
360.378.WINE
www.sanjuanvineyards.com

IN THE EARLY 1890S, THE SAN JUAN COUNTY COMMISSIONER DECREED THAT no child should have to walk or ride a horse over three miles to school. Of the twenty-seven schools built in the County, only two remain today. Sportsman's Lake School now houses the San Juan Islands' only vineyard and winery—San Juan Vineyards. Established in 1996, we now produce over 3000 cases of wine annually.

The vineyard site behind the old school slopes south and is perfectly suited for growing grapes. Because of the cool coastal climate, only certain varieties will ripen here. Our grapes are from the same Northern European latitudes as Northern France and Germany—47°. The harvests are bountiful and include Siegerrebe and Madeleine Angevine. The Siegerrebe makes a semi-dry wine similar to Gewurztraminer. The Madeleine Angevine is dryer and similar to a Pinot Gris.

Our winery complex on Roche Harbor Road processes the estate grown varietals, as well as grapes purchased from vineyards in the Yakima and Columbia valleys. The fall harvest includes picking the grapes from our vineyard, crushing the Merlot, Cabernet and Syrah grapes from Eastern Washington, and fermenting the Chardonnays and the Gewurztraminers.

We welcome guests to our Tasting Room, located in the turn-of-the-century schoolhouse. Our wines are distributed throughout the islands and the Puget Sound, including the Seattle area and the Olympic Peninsula.

Dungeness Crab Cakes with Roasted Pepper Pesto

Caesar Dressing El Gaucho

El Gaucho New York Peppercorn Steak

Bananas Foster

El Gaucho

El Gaucho Restaurant
Paul Mackay,
Owner
John Broulette,
Executive Chef
Nicolas Kassis,
General Manager

2505 1st avenue
seattle, wa 98121
206.728.1337
www.elgaucho.com

El Gaucho is in a class of its own. Harken back to the days of Sinatra and Dean Martin, add low lighting, midnight blue walls, *The Girl from Ipanema* playing on the piano, 28-day dry aged certified Black Angus prime steak and a cigar lounge, and you'll come close to describing El Gaucho.

The crown jewel of Paul Mackay's restaurants, El Gaucho offers handshaken martinis and a silver tray of fruit, nuts, and Rogue River bleu cheese to get you in the mood. Enjoy Wicked Shrimp (shrimp immersed in a butter and beer sauce and spiced with cayenne, chilis, and herbs) before you share a chateaubriand with a tableside preparation of Cliff Sauce (Worcestshire, butter, red wine au jus, and Coleman's mustard). If meat doesn't entice you, order a generous portion of ahi accompanied by wasabi and pickled ginger. Finish your meal with El Gaucho's renowned Bananas Foster prepared tableside.

In addition to the restaurant, El Gaucho offers The 410 Room, a working wine cellar with roundtable seating for as many as eight guests; The Grill Room, your own private club for dinner or receptions; The Wine Cellar, the generously proportioned board-room; The Pampas Room, retro swank and featuring a full dance floor; and The Cigar Lounge, which carries on the tradition of cigar clubs with its overstuffed furniture and celebrity signed memorabilia, the perfect place to enjoy a brandy and cigar.

Dungeness Crab Cakes with Roasted Pepper Pesto

1/4 CUP YELLOW ONION, FINELY MINCED

1/4 CUP CELERY, FINELY MINCED

1 TSP GARLIC, FINELY MINCED

2 TBSP BUTTER, MELTED

1/8 TSP CRUSHED RED PEPPER

1/2 TSP GROUND BLACK PEPPER

1/4 TSP KOSHER SALT

1 CUP HEAVY CREAM

1/4 CUP BEST FOODS MAYONNAISE

1 TBSP DIJON MUSTARD

1 1/2 LB DUNGENESS CRABMEAT, 60/40 MEAT/LEG BLEND

1 CUP PANKO JAPANESE BREADCRUMBS

❖ ROASTED PEPPER PESTO

1 EACH RED, YELLOW, GREEN PEPPER

1/8 CUP FRESH BASIL LEAVES

1/4 CUP PINE NUTS, TOASTED

1/4 CUP VIRGIN OLIVE OIL

SERVES 4 TO 6

In saucepan, sauté onion and garlic in butter until translucent. Add cream and seasoning. Reduce until cream is thickened. Cool for 15 to 20 minutes. Add in mixing bowl—cream mixture, mayonnaise, Dijon mustard, and squeezed crabmeat. Toss with 1/2 cup breadcrumbs. Form into 2 oz balls and flatten to 1/2" thick. Dust each side with remaining breadcrumbs. Pan fry in butter until brown.

❖ Lightly oil peppers. Place on sheet pan in 400° oven. Roast 15 to 20 minutes, turning on all sides. Remove. Cover with food film and cool. Peel off skin and remove stem and seeds. Place in food processor with basil, pine nuts, and olive oil. Coarsely chop until well minced. Serve with crab cakes.

44

Caesar Dressing El Gaucho

SERVES 4-6

Prepare at least 2 hours in advance and refrigerate.

In a food processor or blender, place egg yolks, anchovy, Romano cheese, Dijon mustard, garlic, worchestshire sauce, salt and pepper, and blend on high speed for 2 minutes. Slowly drizzle oil and lemon juice while blending on high speed until all the juice and oil are incorporated.

Wash and chop romaine lettuce, preferably hearts only. You will need 6 to 8 cups for 4 salads depending on preferred size. Toss romaine with 1 oz dressing per cup of romaine. Top with croutons and freshly ground black pepper. Serve.

6-8 CUPS ROMAINE LETTUCE, HEARTS ONLY
4 EGG YOLKS
2 OZ ANCHOVY FILLETS
2 TSP COURSE GROUND PEPPER
3/4 CUP FRESH LEMON JUICE
1/4 CUP ROMANO CHEESE, GRATED
1 1/2 TBSP WORCESTERSHIRE SAUCE
1 CUP EXTRA VIRGIN OLIVE OIL
2 TSP GARLIC, MINCED
1 1/2 TSP KOSHER SALT
2 TBSP DIJON MUSTARD
CROUTONS
FRESHLY GROUND BLACK PEPPER

46

El Gaucho New York Peppercorn Steak

SERVES 4

Prepare peppercorn sauce in advance. Heat charcoal grill or gas grill if charcoal grill is not available.

Pack steaks with cracked pepper and season evenly with steak seasoning. Place on hot grill and sear each side for 4 minutes. Turn.

Each steak should be turned over 3 times after firing for a total of 14 to 16 minutes to reach medium rare to medium, or internal temperature of 115° to 120°. Top with 2 to 3 oz Green Peppercorn Demi Glaze.

❖ Place in saucepan and reduce by half. Add 2 packages or 2 oz More Than Gourmet Brand Beef Demi Glaze with 8 oz of water. Bring to a boil, add roux, whisk, and strain. Add 2 oz green peppercorns.

Finish with 2 tbsp softened butter.

4 16 OZ NEW YORK STEAKS
(PREFERABLY CERTIFIED ANGUS)
8 OZ CRACKED BLACK PEPPERCORNS
1/2 CUP GAUCHO STEAK SEASONING

❖ GREEN PEPPERCORN
DEMI GLAZE
1 TBSP CRACKED BLACK PEPPERCORNS
1/4 TSP CAYENNE PEPPER
1/8 TSP GROUND WHITE PEPPER
1/2 TSP SUGAR
1 TBSP ROUX
4 OZ BURGUNDY WINE
(SUBSTITUTE CABERNET)

47

Bananas Foster

SERVES 4

Melt butter in flambé pan or attractive skillet. Add sugar and mix with butter in pan. Squeeze in juice of 1/2 lemon. Remove from heat and add Banana Liqueur. Heat again. Flambe with 1/2 to 1 oz rum.

Place bananas on dessert plates in circle around vanilla ice cream. Spoon hot sauce over bananas and ice cream. Serve.

1 TBSP BUTTER
2 BANANAS, CUT IN HALF
LENGTHWISE
3/4 CUP BROWN SUGAR
1/2 LEMON
2 TBSPS BANANA LIQUEUR
2 SCOOPS VANILLA ICE CREAM
1 OZ RUM

Wine Pairing

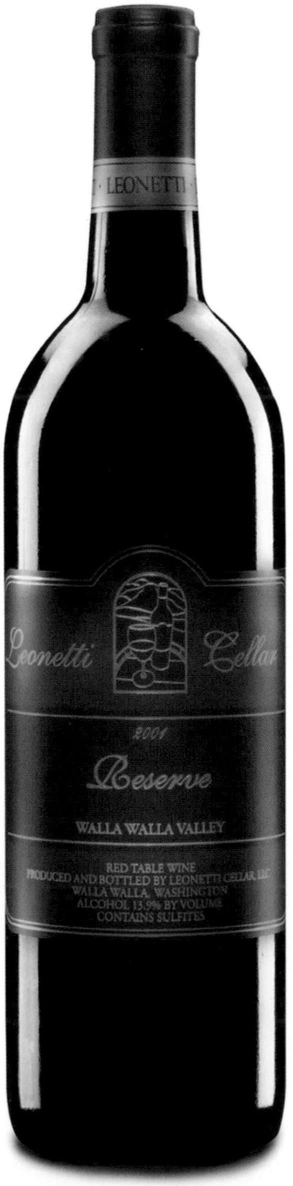

Dungeness Crab Cakes with Roasted Pepper Pesto
2002 Sangiovese
Walla Walla Valley

Caesar Dressing El Gaucho
2002 Merlot
Columbia Valley

El Gaucho New York Peppercorn Steak
2001 Cabernet Sauvignon
Walla Walla Valley

Bananas Foster
2001 Reserve
Walla Walla Valley

2001

Reserve

WALLA WALLA VALLEY

RED TABLE WINE
PRODUCED AND BOTTLED BY LEONETTI CELLAR, LLC
WALLA WALLA, WASHINGTON
ALCOHOL 13.9% BY VOLUME
CONTAINS SULFITES

LEONETTI
CELLAR

FIGGINS FAMILY,
OWNER

1875 FOOTHILLS LANE

WALLA WALLA, WA 99362

509.525.1428

www.leonetticellar.com

LEONETTI CELLAR IS THE OLDEST WINERY IN THE WALLA WALLA VALLEY. In 1977, inspired by his Italian heritage, Gary Figgins fulfilled his lifelong dream to become a winemaker. More than a quarter century later, Gary and Nancy Figgins maintain their dedication to "no compromise" winemaking in their quest to produce the finest Cabernet Sauvignon, Merlot, and Sangiovese in the world.

The winery boasts four distinctly sighted Estate Vineyards—Mill Creek Upland, Loess, Estate (winery) block, and Seven Hills. Each contributes distinct characteristics to the Leonetti label.

Gary's son Chris, who grew up watching the business mature, joined the winery full-time in 1996. The father and son team are dedicated to the pursuit of quality. This dedication is reflected in their decisions—from the vineyard site location, viticultural management, and winemaking process to air drying custom-cut stave wood on the Estate, ensuring only the best cooperage enters the cellar.

Leonetti's wines are described as "hedonistic delights"—always intense, layered with ripe fruit and spice, balanced for longevity, with flavors imbued by the judicious use of oak.

Exciting to drink by itself, each wine reaches its true height when accompanying a fine meal.

Flash Grilled Calamari and Red Wine Braised Octopus with

Roasted Pepper Ragu, White Beans, and Fresh Oregano

Bibb Salad with Hazelnut Vinaigrette and a Shower of Oregonzola Bleu Cheese

Spiced Tuna Steak Seared Rare with Sweet and Sour Slaw, Charmoula Yogurt, and Chickpea Mash

Goat Cheese Cake and Lemon-thyme Shortbread

FISH CLUB
IN THE MARRIOTT HOTEL
CHRIS AINSWORTH,
EXECUTIVE CHEF
VALERIE MUDRY,
PASTRY CHEF

THE NEW FISH CLUB, A RESTAURANT BY TODD ENGLISH, AT SEATTLE'S waterside Marriott Hotel was inspired by the fishing traditions of the Mediterranean, where fisherman gathered after their time at sea to trade stories, share food and drink, and celebrate their catch. The restaurant is in the swim as it provides fresh seafood and fare reminiscent of Mediterranean cafés. From Pacific Cod Osso Bucco to Whole Trout and Harissa Barbequed Leg of Lamb, the international menu is served by professionals on dishware customized to the meal.

Chef Chris Ainsworth, once the protégé of celebrity chef Todd English at his Miramar and Bonfire restaurants on the East Coast, now holds his own as the big fish at Fish Club. Entrée by entrée, Chris's culinary creations have endeared themselves to reviewers and diners eager for a taste of the sea (and land) as they "trade stories, share food and drink, and celebrate," watching the ships come in and out of Puget Sound.

1800 ALASKAN WAY

SEATTLE, WA 98121

206.256.1040

www.toddenglish.com/

restaurants/fishclub.html

Flash Grilled Calamari and
Red Wine Braised Octopus with Roasted Pepper Ragu, White Beans, and Fresh Oregano

1 LB SQUID TUBE, CUT IN HALF

SERVES 4

❖ BRAISED OCTOPUS
1 1-2 LB BABY OCTOPUS, WHOLE
1 BOTTLE RED WINE
1 BUNCH FRESH THYME
1 BAY LEAF
1 TSP PEPPERCORNS
1/4 CUP CARROT, CHOPPED
1/4 CUP ONION, CHOPPED
1/4 CUP CELERY, CHOPPED

❖ WHITE BEANS
2 CUPS WHITE BEANS,
SOAKED OVERNIGHT IN WATER* AND
STRAINED (IF BEANS ARE NOT SOAKED,
ALLOW FOR MORE COOKING TIME)
1 LB PANCETTA BACON, DICED
(OR REGULAR BACON, IF DESIRED)
1/4 CUP CARROT, DICED
1/4 CUP ONION, DICED
1/4 CUP CELERY, DICED
*Chicken broth can be substituted
for water for extra flavor.*

❖ ROASTED PEPPER RAGU
3 RED PEPPERS, ROASTED, PEELED,
DESEEDED, AND DICED
3 ANAHEIM PEPPERS, ROASTED, PEELED,
DESEEDED, AND DICED
1/4 CUP GARLIC, ROASTED
AND CHOPPED
1/4 CUP EXTRA VIRGIN OLIVE OIL
1/4 CUP WHITE WINE
1 BUNCH FRESH OREGANO,
PICKED AND ROUGH CHOPPED
(RESERVE 2 WHOLE SPRIGS FOR GARNISH)
RED CHILI FLAKES TO TASTE
2 LEMONS, JUICED

❖ Octopus can be made a day in advance if desired.

Combine all ingredients into small pot and bring to a simmer. Cover and let cook for 2 to 3 hours or until tender. Strain ingredients from liquid and cool. Remove tentacles and reserve.

❖ Beans can be made 1 day in advance if desired and reheated when needed.

Render pancetta bacon over low heat until just turning golden. Add vegetables and sweat over medium high heat until soft, about 2 minutes. Add soaked beans and continue to sweat for about 2 minutes. Cover with water and simmer until very tender, about 1 hour or more, if needed. Reserve for later.

❖ Heat a medium to large sauté pan. Add extra virgin olive oil. Sweat garlic and peppers. Add chili flakes, white wine, and lemon juice. Add more olive oil, if desired. Finish with fresh oregano. Taste and adjust to personal preference for spice and flavor.

The sauce should be like a warm, spicy, roasted pepper vinaigrette.

ASSEMBLY
Season and grill squid tubes and octopus tentacles for 2 to 3 minutes. Warm white beans and place in center of plate or platter. Arrange squid and octopus on white beans. Top with ragu. Garnish with sprig of oregano. Serve.

52

*Bibb Salad with Hazelnut Vinaigrette and
a Shower of Oregonzola Bleu Cheese*

53

SERVES 4

Gently clean lettuce by removing the core and picking the stems. Wash and gently let dry. Rough chop toasted hazelnuts and combine with hazelnut oil. Gently toss lettuce in bowl with a little olive oil, lemon juice, and salt and pepper. Stack on plate. Top with a spoonful of hazelnut and oil mixture. Add a pinch of red onion.

Generously grate Oregonzola cheese over salad with fine grater for Moulin. Garnish with a bunch of Mâche and serve.

2 HEADS BOSTON BIBB LETTUCE
1/2 CUP HAZELNUTS, TOASTED
8-10 OZ OREGONZOLA BLEU CHEESE, CUT INTO SMALL BLOCKS AND FROZEN
1/4 CUP HAZELNUT OIL
1/4 CUP BALSAMIC VINEGAR
1/4 CUP EXTRA VIRGIN OLIVE OIL
1/2 RED ONION, SHAVED THIN
4 BUNCHES MÂCHE OR LAMBS LETTUCE
FRESH SQUEEZED LEMON JUICE, TO TASTE
SALT AND PEPPER

Spiced Tuna Steak Seared Rare with Sweet and Sour Slaw, Charmoula Yogurt, and Chick Pea Mash

❖ TUNA STEAK

2 1/2 LB #1 GRADE TUNA,
CUT INTO 8 OZ PORTIONS
1 TBSP CORIANDER SEED, WHOLE
1 TBSP CARDAMOM PODS, WHOLE
1 STICK CINNAMON
2 TSP CUMIN SEED, WHOLE
2 TSP PEPPERCORN, WHOLE

❖ CHICK PEA MASH

1 LB DRIED CHICK PEAS OR GARBANZO
BEANS, SOAKED OVERNIGHT
AND STRAINED
1/4 CUP EXTRA VIRGIN OLIVE OIL
SALT AND PEPPER
1 CUP CHICKEN BROTH

❖ SWEET AND
SOUR SLAW

1/2 HEAD CABBAGE
2 CARROTS
1 LARGE RED ONION, CUT JULIENNE
1/2 CUP SUGAR
1/2 CUP WHITE WINE VINEGAR
1 BUNCH FRESH THYME, PICKED CLEAN
1/4-1/2 CUP CHICKEN BROTH
SALT AND PEPPER

❖ CHARMOULA YOGURT

1 BUNCH FRESH CILANTRO, CHOPPED
1/2 BUNCH FRESH
FLAT LEAF PARSLEY, CHOPPED
1 TSP LEMON ZEST
1 TSP GROUND CUMIN SEED
3 CLOVES GARLIC, MINCED
3/4 CUP EXTRA VIRGIN OLIVE OIL
2-3 FRESH CHILIS, SEEDED AND MINCED
1/4 CUP FRESH LEMON JUICE
1/2 CUP PLAIN YOGURT

SERVES 4

❖ Toast all dried spices over medium high heat in small sauté pan until aromatic, about 2 minutes. Grind spices in blender or coffee grinder until fine. Reserve.

❖ Cook chick peas in water until very tender, about 1 hour or more if not soaked. Strain water and stir mash adding olive oil, chicken broth, and salt and pepper to desired consistency and taste. A splash of lemon juice can be added to brighten the flavor, if desired. Its consistency should spread over the plate or platter but should not run.

❖ Shred the cabbage, carrots, and onion like you would for coleslaw, but keep them separate. In a large pan over high heat, add a little olive oil. Sauté the onions for about 1 1/2 minutes. Add carrots and cook for 2 more minutes. Add cabbage and cook for 2 more minutes. Stir in sugar. Add thyme, vinegar, and broth. Cook for 2 more minutes. Season with salt and pepper. The taste should be a balanced sweet and sour. The texture should still be slightly crisp.

❖ Combine all ingredients except for yogurt in a food processor. Blend in short bursts to a rough purée. Season to taste. Stir purée into yogurt. The yogurt should help to blend and balance the flavors, adding its own subtle touch.

ASSEMBLY

Season tuna with spice rub. Salt and pepper liberally. Sear tuna in cast iron pan or sauté pan over high heat. Cook about 1 1/2 minutes per side. Remove tuna and slice in half, showing off the beautiful red center. Place hot chick pea mash in center of platter. Arrange tuna on the bed of chick peas. Top tuna with warm sweet and sour slaw. Spoon charmoula yogurt around the outside of the dish. Garnish with a smattering of fresh picked cilantro.

54

Goat Cheese Cakes

SERVES 4 · 8 2 1/2 " RAMEKINS OR RING MOLDS

Preheat oven to 325°.

12 OZ GOOD QUALITY GOAT CHEESE
(LAURA CHENEL, FRENCH COUTERIER)

If using ring molds, wrap the bottom and sides tightly with aluminum foil. Spray interior of molds or ramekins with food-release spray. Sprinkle interiors and sides with superfine sugar. Tap out excess. Place prepared molds or ramekins in 2 1/2" or deeper cake pan. Place goat cheese, sugar, lemon zest, and nutmeg in food processor. Blend until smooth. Add eggs, one at a time, blending completely after each addition. Pour in heavy cream. Scrape down sides and bottom of bowl and blend until smooth.

2/3 CUP SUPERFINE SUGAR
ZEST OF ONE LEMON, FINELY GRATED
1/4 TSP NUTMEG, FINELY GRATED
3 WHOLE EGGS
1/4 CUP HEAVY CREAM

Pour batter evenly into molds or ramekins. Pour warm water into cake pan around the molds (water bath) and bake at 325° uncovered for 18 to 25 minutes. Centers of cheesecakes will be set and edges will be a very light golden brown. When cooled, remove ramekins from the water bath and refrigerate until cooled completely.

To serve, release cheesecakes from molds or turn out of ramekins. I like to sprinkle the tops of the cheesecakes with turbinado (raw) sugar and caramelize them with a blowtorch. This forms a crispy crust like a crème brûlée. Serve with lemon-thyme shortbread (*recipe follows*) and seasonal fruits like poached pears, red grapes, figs, and roasted apricots.

Lemon-thyme Shortbread

2 DOZEN COOKIES

1 LB UNSALTED EUROPEAN-STYLE
BUTTER, SOFTENED

Preheat oven to 325°.

1 CUP SUPERFINE SUGAR

Using the paddle attachment of your hand mixer or stand mixer, cream together softened butter and sugar until light and fluffy. Add lemon zest and mix until blended. Add the flour, salt, pepper, and lemon thyme and mix just until the dough is blended. Remove it from the mixing bowl and pat into a rectangle. Wrap the dough in plastic and let it rest in the refrigerator for about 1 hour.

ZEST OF 1 LEMON, FINELY GRATED
4 CUPS ALL-PURPOSE FLOUR
1/3 TSP KOSHER SALT
1 TSP GROUND BLACK PEPPER
3 TBSP LEMON THYME,
FINELY CHOPPED

Roll out the rested shortbread to approximately 1/8" thick. You can use a floured countertop and brush off the excess flour or roll the dough between sheets of parchment. Chill. Once the dough is cold, the parchment will peel right off and the dough is ready to cut. Use a cookie cutter to cut the dough into desired shapes. Place on parchment lined baking sheets. (Dough scraps can be rolled once more!) Sprinkle with superfine sugar and bake for 7 to 10 minutes. The outside edges of the shortbread will be a light golden brown when done.

Flash Grilled Calamari and Red Wine Braised Octopus
with Roasted Pepper Ragu, White Beans,
and Fresh Oregano
Yakima Valley Cabernet Franc

Bibb Salad with Hazelnut Vinaigrette
and a Shower of Oregonzola Bleu Cheese
Yakima Valley Cabernet Franc Rose

Spiced Tuna Steak Seared Rare with Sweet and Sour Slaw,
Charmoula Yogurt, and Chickpea Mash
Yakima Valley Semillon or Yakima Valley Merlot

Goat Cheese Cakes and Lemon-thyme Shortbread
Yakima Valley Sauvignon Blanc

56

CHINOOK
WINES

KAY SIMON AND CLAY MACKEY,
OWNERS

PO BOX 387

PROSSER, WA 99350

509.786.2725

www.chinookwines.com

IN 1983, KAY SIMON AND CLAY MACKEY COMBINED THEIR EXTENSIVE experience in winemaking and viticulture to form Chinook Wines. As pioneers in the early growth of the Washington State wine industry, theirs was a perfect marriage. Though Kay and Clay have joked that one of them should have married rich, their winery is truly a testimonial to a winning partnership.

Chinook wines have become synonymous with highly acclaimed wines produced from Chardonnay, Sauvignon Blanc, Semillon, Merlot, Cabernet Franc, and Cabernet Sauvignon grapes, reflecting the finest attributes of Washington State wines.

Bounded by a Cabernet Franc vineyard and apple and cherry orchards, the winery is a favorite stop on the Yakima Valley winetasting trail. Original farm buildings house the winery, barrel storage, and tasting room and a shaded lawn serves as a picnic area and backdrop for enjoying the best of Chinook wines.

Butter Poached Spot Prawns, Roast Potato Ravioli & New Morels

Georgian Heirloom Tomato Terrine

Mustard Roasted Rack of Lamb with Mint Fava Bean Pesto

Cabernet Stained Pears with Brie Ice Cream

The Georgian

THE GEORGIAN
THE FAIRMONT
OLYMPIC HOTEL,
SEATTLE,
OWNER
GAVIN STEPHENSON,
EXECUTIVE CHEF

411 UNIVERSITY STREET
SEATTLE, WA 98101
206.621.7889
www.fairmont.com/seattle

THE GEORGIAN IS THE CROWN JEWEL OF THE FAIRMONT OLYMPIC, SEATTLE's most elegant hotel. Boasting ornate ceilings, dazzling chandeliers, and fifteen–foot Palladian windows, The Georgian makes visitors feel as though they have just stepped inside an exquisite, light–filled Fabergé egg.

The spectacular menu provides its own visual delights, with an emphasis on exquisite presentation. Executive Chef Gavin Stephenson showcases seasonal Pacific Northwest ingredients prepared in classic French style. His creations include Dungeness Crab Bisque infused with tarragon and cognac garnished with Mini Crab Cakes; Persillade Crusted Rack of Lamb with Basil and Goat Cheese Puréed Potatoes and Ratatouille Sauce; and White and Dark Chocolate Soufflé. The extensive wine list satisfies the broad tastes of The Georgian's cosmopolitan guests, featuring an extraordinary selection of French wines among a wide array of world–class wines, with special attention to labels from Washington and Oregon. The knowledgeable wait staff is attentive while masterfully unobtrusive.

The Georgian epitomizes sophistication, yet it has none of the stuffiness one might encounter in a similar restaurant in a more formal city. It is not unusual to glance around the grand dining room and see a variety of diners reveling in The Georgian's charm: a group of business people, a couple celebrating a romantic occasion, or a more casual gathering of friends.

The Georgian is repeatedly rated in Zagat Survey as one of Seattle's best restaurants. In both 2002 and 2003, *Food and Wine* named The Georgian one of America's Top 50 Hotel restaurants.

Butter Poached Spot Prawns,
Roast Potato Ravioli & New Morels

12 LARGE FRESH SPOT PRAWNS, PEELED
2 CUPS CLARIFIED BUTTER

SERVES 4

❖ Start by making the pasta dough. In a mixer with a dough hook, combine all the dough ingredients. Mix on a medium low speed for 15 minutes until the dough feels supple. Allow to rest for 30 minutes before using.

❖ RAVIOLI FILLING
2 LARGE YUKON GOLD POTATOES, COOKED IN SALTED WATER
3 SHALLOTS, DICED FINE
2 CLOVES OF GARLIC, CRUSHED
1/2 TSP FRESH THYME, CHOPPED
1 TBSP PARSLEY, CHOPPED
2 TBSP BUTTER

Make the ravioli filling by cutting the potatoes into 1/2" pieces and sauté with the butter until they start to brown. Add the shallots and garlic and sauté until they are clear and have no more "raw" flavor. Transfer mixture to a bowl and mash with a fork. Add thyme and parsley. Mix well.

PASTA DOUGH
2 CUPS BREAD FLOUR
1/4 CUP SEMOLINA
3 EGGS, BEATEN
1 TBSP OLIVE OIL
1 TSP SALT

Roll the pasta dough into thin sheets. Place a sheet over a ravioli rack. Fill each pocket with some potato filling and lay another sheet over it. Roll with a rolling pin and pop the ravioli out. Makes 1 dozen ravioli.

Warm the clarified butter to 130 ° in a saucepan. In another pot, bring 1 qt of water to a boil for the ravioli.

❖ THE MORELS
8 OZ FRESH MORELS, WASHED AND DRIED
2 SHALLOTS, DICED FINE
1 GARLIC CLOVE
1 1/2 CUPS CHICKEN STOCK
6 TBSP BUTTER

❖ Start the morels by heating 2 tbsp of butter in a sauté pan and sauté until all the water has left the mushrooms. Add the shallots and garlic and sauté for 1 1/2 minutes longer. Add the stock and reduce until 1/2 cup of liquid remains. Season with salt and pepper. Remove from the heat and stir in 4 tbsp of butter. Keep warm.

Poach the prawns by submerging them in the hot clarified butter. Add salt and pepper. Cook for 4 to 4 1/2 minutes. While the prawns are cooking, plunge the ravioli into the boiling salted water. Cook for 4 to 5 minutes. Drain well and toss with a small amount of butter.

ASSEMBLY

Assemble the dish by spooning the mushroom mixture onto 4 plates. Place 3 ravioli on top of the mushrooms and a spot prawn on top of each ravioli. Garnish with fresh picked herbs. Serve immediately.

Georgian Heirloom Tomato Terrine

SERVES 4

16 LARGE HEIRLOOM TOMATOES, MIXED VARIETY

36 BASIL LEAVES

1 LARGE TRUFFLE

2 TBSP TRUFFLE OIL

1/4 CUP BALSAMIC VINEGAR

SALT AND PEPPER

To peel tomatoes, cut a shallow "X" into the bottom of each tomato and plunge them into rapidly boiling water for 15 seconds. Remove and immediately plunge into ice water until cool. When cool, peel off skins with sharp knife. Quarter tomatoes and filet by cutting seeds away from tomato flesh. (You can reserve inside for gazpacho or tomato sauce.) Set aside.

❖ BALSAMIC VINAIGRETTE

1 TBSP DIJON MUSTARD

1 TBSP HONEY

2 TBSP BALSAMIC VINEGAR

PINCH OF SALT AND PEPPER

SLOWLY WHISK IN 1/2 CUP OLIVE OIL

Spray small terrine or loaf pan with non-stick spray and place plastic wrap inside making sure there are no air bubbles and enough wrap to cover terrine when finished layering.

Build terrine by placing tomato filets along bottom of pan, making sure they overlap slightly. To make terrine decorative, use only like colors of tomato filets for each layer. Be sure to lightly season each layer of tomato with salt and pepper. Lay basil leaves between every third layer.

When terrine or pan is full, bring edges of the plastic wrap over to cover terrine. With a sharp knife, poke several holes in the plastic wrap. Place a baking sheet on top of the terrine and flip terrine and pan upside down. Refrigerate. Allow to drain. Set for 4 to 6 hours.

❖ To serve terrine, remove from loaf pan. Leaving plastic on, carefully slice 3/4 to 1" slices with a very sharp knife. Place each slice carefully on a plate and remove plastic. Garnish with a drizzle of truffle oil, balsamic vinaigrette, shaved truffle, and basil sprigs.

61

Mustard Roasted Rack of Lamb
with Mint Fava Bean Pesto

2 DOUBLE RACK OF LAMB,
FAT CAP REMOVED AND
BONES "FRENCHED"
SALT AND PEPPER
1/2 CUP DIJON MUSTARD
1 TSP THYME, CHOPPED
1/2 CUP PARSLEY, CHOPPED
2 CUPS BREAD CRUMBS
1/4 CUP CANOLA OIL

❖ PESTO
1/2 LB FRESH FAVA BEANS
(ABOUT 4 LB WHOLE PODS)
1/4 CUP MINT LEAVES
1/4 CUP PARSLEY LEAVES
2 OZ PARMESAN, GRATED
1/3 CUP OLIVE OIL
SALT AND PEPPER

SERVES 4

Heat a sauté pan until very hot. Season the lamb with salt and pepper. Put the oil in the pan and sear the lamb on all sides. Remove from the pan and coat with the Dijon mustard. Combine thyme, parsley, and breadcrumbs. Coat lamb with the mixture. Place the coated racks on a baking sheet.

Heat oven to 375°. Roast the lamb for 30 to 35 minutes or until it reaches an internal temperature of 125° (medium).

❖ While the lamb is roasting, make the pesto. In a food processor, combine all of the ingredients but 20 of the fava beans that will be used as garnish. Purée all the ingredients into a paste. The pesto should be slightly runny.

When lamb is ready, remove from the oven and allow to rest for 10 minutes.

Carve the lamb into chops and arrange on 4 plates. With a spoon, drizzle some pesto onto each plate. Sprinkle the reserved fava beans onto the plate. Serve at once. Excellent with boiled or roasted new potatoes.

62

Cabernet Stained Pears with Brie Ice Cream

SERVES 4

4 BOSC PEARS, PEELED AND CORED
2 BOTTLES CABERNET SAUVIGNON
1 STAR ANISE
3 CLOVES
4 CUPS SUGAR

Mix together wine, sugar, and spices. Place the pears standing up in a pot. Cover with the wine, sugar, and spice mixture and bring to a simmer. Simmer slowly for approximately 1 hour or until pears are soft. Do not allow the pears to boil. Cool the pears in the liquid to retain maximum flavor and color.

✦ FROZEN BRIE
1 LB 8 OZ BRIE
3 CUPS SIMPLE SYRUP

Once the pears are cool, remove from the syrup. Reduce the syrup until it is very thick. Cool. This is the sauce for the dessert.

To present the dessert, place each pear on a plate with a scoop of the frozen Brie. With a squirt bottle or tines of a fork, drizzle the pear syrup over the Brie and the pear. Serve immediately.

✦ Make by combining 2 cups water with 2 cups sugar. Bring to boil and cool. Add 1/4 cup water to simple syrup.

63

Open Brie and scrape out the soft part of the cheese. Discard cheese rind. Slowly add simple syrup into Brie, whisking gently until mixture is creamy. Strain until there are no cheese lumps in the mixture. Freeze mixture in sorbet or ice cream machine. Scoop onto plate next to pear, or cut into wedges held together with thin slices of white chocolate.

Wine Pairing

BUTTER POACHED SPOT PRAWNS, ROAST POTATO RAVIOLI & NEW MORELS
2001 REININGER MERLOT
WALLA WALLA VALLEY

GEORGIAN HEIRLOOM TOMATO TERRINE
1999 REININGER CIMA
WALLA WALLA VALLEY,
50% SANGIOVESE, 25% CABERNET SAUVIGNON, & 25% MERLOT

MUSTARD ROASTED RACK OF LAMB WITH MINT FAVA BEAN PESTO
2001 REININGER SYRAH
WALLA WALLA VALLEY

CABERNET STAINED PEARS WITH BRIE ICE CREAM
2000 REININGER CABERNET SAUVIGNON
WALLA WALLA VALLEY

64

REININGER WINES ARE A MARRIAGE OF SEVERAL vineyards and grape varieties that create a true expression of the Walla Walla Valley. I strive to find uniqueness throughout the valley and meticulously vinify, maturate, and assemble wines to experience the whole. "Listening" to the fruit, intuition, gentle handling of fruit and wine, patience, and a belief that individual vineyard blocks require separate approaches with every vintage both in the vineyard and in the winery, culminate to weave the valley's maternal elements within the fruit into an elegant, finely structured expression of the Walla Walla Valley that is the hallmark of Reininger wines.

Reininger Winery blossomed in 1997 from my home winemaking experience. My wife Tracy and I established our "shackteau" in a tiny tin building at the airport. In 2003, we realized we'd outgrown our humble beginnings and, with the help of Tracy's brothers and parents, began the renovation of two agricultural buildings on seven acres four miles west of Walla Walla. Surrounded by wheat fields and small farms, we will continue our tradition of vinifying Cabernet Sauvignon, Syrah, Merlot, Malbec, Carmenere, Petit Verdot, and Sangiovese.

REININGER
WINERY

CHUCK & TRACY REININGER,
JAY AND CYNDI TUCKER, AND
KELLY & ANN TUCKER,
OWNERS

5858 W HIGHWAY 12
WALLA WALLA, WA 99362
509.522.1994
www.reiningerwinery.com

We're proud of our consistent, outstanding quality. Our wines have earned gold medal recognition at the San Francisco International Wine Competition, Pacific NW Enological Society Grand Award, and three Wine Press Northwest Platinums (a judging of Northwest gold medal wines).

My inspiration comes from the valley itself. My passion for winemaking stems from a profound reverence for the awesome and sometimes cataclysmic forces that shape our world. For me, the process is an adventure of the soul and of mother earth. The wonder is in the journey, the joy is in the sharing.

Enjoy the simple pleasure of savoring the complexities!
—Chuck Reininger, Winemaker

Carrot Ravioli and King Bolete Mushrooms with Currants, Fried Sage and Sage Blossoms

Stinging Nettle and Mussel Soup with Lovage

Slow-Roasted Wild King Salmon with Peas and Lemon Thyme

Pumpkin-Bay Soufflé with Orange Thyme Custard Sauce

The Herbfarm

THE HERBFARM
RON ZIMMERMAN AND
CARRIE VAN DYCK,
OWNERS
JERRY TRAUNFELD,
EXECUTIVE CHEF

14590 NE 145TH STREET

WOODINVILLE, WA 98072

425.485.5300

www.theherbfarm.com

THE HERBFARM IS ONE OF AMERICA'S UNIQUE DINING EXPERIENCES. With each visit to The Herbfarm, you'll delight in a multi-course set menu, which showcases both the food and the wines of the Pacific Northwest. The restaurant creates a culinary sense of place and time through the progression of the local foods served each day. The nightly nine-course dinner lasts about four and a half hours and includes six wines carefully paired to the food.

Yards of billowing fabric swath the heavy-timbered dining room where chandeliers float in space below the soaring ceiling. The tables glitter with Riedel stemware and Christofle flatware and are animated by candles and the faces of happy guests. An army of gracious servers seamlessly tends your every care. Music flows from the guitar of Spanish maestro Patricio Contreras.

Nationally renowned Chef Jerry Traunfeld won the James Beard Award for "Best American Chef, Northwest." The restaurant is one of only fifty in America with the AAA 5-Diamond Award.

The Herbfarm awaits you in the middle of a farm valley about twenty minutes from downtown Seattle. The restaurant also has overnight suites that have been lavished with original art and antiques collected from throughout the world.

This is a one-of-a-kind destination. Reservations should be made in advance, though last-minute cancellations may allow you to gain a table on the day of service.

Carrot Ravioli and King Bolete Mushrooms with Currants, Fried Sage and Sage Blossoms

❖ CARROT RAVIOLI

3/4 LB CARROTS, PEELED AND
COARSELY CHOPPED
3 TBSP UNSALTED BUTTER
1 LEEK, FINELY CHOPPED
1 TSP CORIANDER SEED, GROUND
1/2 TSP FRESH GINGER, GRATED
1/2 CUP WHOLE MILK RICOTTA CHEESE
SALT AND PEPPER TO TASTE
1/2 LB FRESH PASTA DOUGH
EGG WASH

2 TBSP EXTRA VIRGIN OLIVE OIL
1 1/2 LB FRESH BOLETUS EDULIS
MUSHROOMS (ALSO CALLED PORCINI
OR CEPE), BRUSHED CLEAN
AND SLICED IN WEDGES
1 TBSP SHALLOT, FINELY CHOPPED
1 TSP GARLIC, FINELY CHOPPED
1 CUP DRY WHITE WINE
2 CUPS RICH CHICKEN STOCK
1 TBSP UNSALTED BUTTER
1 TBSP FRESH MARJORAM,
COARSELY CHOPPED
4 CUPS VEGETABLE OIL FOR DEEP FRYING
40 FRESH SAGE LEAVES
3 TBSP DRIED CURRANTS,
PLUMPED IN HOT WATER
SAGE BLOSSOMS

SERVES 8

❖ For the ravioli, boil the carrots in a large pot of salted water until tender. Drain. Melt the butter in a medium sized saucepan. Add the leek, coriander, and ginger. Cook until softened but not browned, about 8 minutes. Stir in the carrots and ricotta. Purée the mixture in a food processor, leaving some texture. Season with salt and pepper.

Roll the pasta into two very thin sheets. Brush the bottom sheet with egg wash. Arrange 24 1 tbsp–sized mounds of filling on the bottom sheet. Top with the second sheet, pressing out all air bubbles. Cut out the ravioli with a 2" cutter.

Heat the olive oil over medium high heat in a large skillet. Add the mushrooms, season with salt, and cook while tossing until well browned. Add the shallot and garlic, cook briefly, and then lower the heat and add the wine. When the liquid is nearly evaporated, add the stock and continue to simmer until the mushrooms are soft and the sauce is slightly thickened. Swirl in the butter and marjoram and season with additional salt and pepper.

Heat the vegetable oil to 350°. Drop in the sage leaves and cook until they stop sizzling, about 15 seconds. Lift from the oil, drain on paper towel, and season with salt.

Arrange 3 ravioli and 3 mushroom wedges on each of 8 plates. Drizzle with some of the mushroom sauce. Sprinkle with the currants, fried sage, and sage blossoms.

Stinging Nettle and Mussel Soup with Lovage

SERVES 6

4 OZ YOUNG STINGING NETTLE LEAVES
(HANDLE WITH GLOVES WHEN RAW)

2 LB SMALL LIVE MUSSELS

1/2 CUP DRY WHITE WINE

2 TBSP BUTTER

2 CUPS LEEK, THINLY SLICED

2 CUPS CHICKEN STOCK

1 TBSP WHITE RICE

1/4 CUP YOUNG LOVAGE LEAVES

SALT AND FRESHLY GROUND
BLACK PEPPER

CRÈME FRAÎCHE FOR GARNISH

Boil the nettles in a large pot of salted boiling water for 2 minutes. Drain, rinse under cold water, and squeeze dry.

Put the mussels and wine in a large pot with a tight fitting lid. Place over high heat until the mussels open, about 4 minutes. Drain the mussels, reserving the liquid, and remove the meat from the shells. You should have about 2 cups liquid. If there is less, add chicken stock to come to 2 cups.

Cook the leek in the butter over medium heat in a large saucepan until softened. Add the mussel liquid, chicken stock, and rice. Cover and cook at an even simmer for about 30 minutes, or until the rice is very soft. Stir in the lovage and the blanched nettles. Purée the soup in small batches in a blender until very smooth. Return to the pan and bring it back to a simmer. Taste and add pepper and additional salt, if needed. Stir in the reserved mussels. Ladle into warm bowls and drizzle with crème fraîche.

Slow-Roasted Wild King Salmon with Peas and Lemon Thyme

❧ SALMON

8 4 OZ PIECES WILD KING SALMON
FILLET, SKINNED AND
PIN BONES REMOVED
1/4 CUP EXTRA VIRGIN OLIVE OIL
FINE SEA SALT

❧ SAUCE

1/2 CUP DRY WHITE WINE
2 TBSP SHALLOT, FINELY CHOPPED
1 TBSP LEMON JUICE
3 TBSP UNSALTED BUTTER
1 TBSP LEMON THYME,
COARSELY CHOPPED
SALT AND FRESHLY GROUND PEPPER

2 TBSP UNSALTED BUTTER
1 1/2 CUPS SNOW OR SNAP PEAS,
BLANCHED
4 CUPS PEA SPROUTS OR PEA VINES
COARSE SEA SALT
PEA BLOSSOMS

SERVES 8

❧ Preheat a convection oven to 200°. Lay the salmon on a baking sheet that was brushed with some of the olive oil, and brush the remaining oil on the fish. Season lightly with the sea salt. Bake for 20 to 30 minutes or until the fish flakes very slightly when pressed on, but is still slightly translucent and deeply colored.

❧ For the sauce, bring the white wine, shallots, and lemon juice to a simmer in a small saucepan and continue to cook until it is reduced to half the volume. Whisk in the 3 tbsp butter, 1 tbsp at a time. Stir in the lemon thyme. Season with salt and pepper.

Melt the remaining butter in a large skillet. Add the blanched peas and cook until warmed through. Add the pea sprouts, season with salt, and cook until just wilted.

Arrange the peas and sprouts on warm dinner plates. Sprinkle a little coarse salt on the salmon fillets and place them on top of the sprouts. Pour the sauce around the fish and garnish with pea blossoms.

Pumpkin-Bay Soufflé with Orange Thyme Custard Sauce

SERVES 8

SOFT BUTTER AND SUGAR FOR
PREPARING THE RAMEKINS

1 1/2 CUPS MILK

8 FRESH BAY LAUREL LEAVES
(NOT CALIFORNIA BAY)

1/2 VANILLA BEAN, SPLIT

4 LARGE EGG YOLKS

3/4 CUP SUGAR

5 TBSP ALL PURPOSE FLOUR

1 CUP PUMPKIN PURÉE (IF USING
FRESH PUMPKIN PURÉE, DRAIN IN
CHEESECLOTH OVERNIGHT)

8 LARGE EGG WHITES

Generously butter the interiors of 8 6 oz ramekins and coat them with sugar. Arrange them in a shallow baking dish.

Heat the milk in a medium saucepan. When it boils, add the bay leaves, lightly crushed, and the vanilla bean, then turn off the heat and let steep for 20 minutes. Strain the milk and return it to the pan.

Beat the egg yolks with 6 tbsp of the sugar in a large mixing bowl. Whisk in the flour, then the hot milk. Transfer the mixture back into the saucepan and whisk over medium heat until it boils and thickens. Scoop the mixture back to the mixing bowl and whisk in the pumpkin purée.

❧ ORANGE THYME
CUSTARD SAUCE

2 CUPS MILK

4 3" SPRIGS FRESH THYME

GRATED ZEST OF 1/2 ORANGE

6 LARGE EGG YOLKS

1/2 CUP SUGAR

When ready to bake the soufflés, preheat the oven to 375°. Beat the egg whites in an electric mixer until they begin to turn white. Slowly beat in the remaining 6 tbsp of sugar and continue to beat until they form stiff peaks but remain glossy. Fold 1/3 of the egg whites into the pumpkin base, then gently fold in the remaining. Fill the ramekins to the top. Pour about 1" of hot water into the baking dish and bake the soufflés for about 20 to 25 minutes or until they rise high above the rims and begin to turn golden brown. Serve immediately with pitchers of the sauce.

❧ Bring the milk to a boil in a small saucepan. Stir in the thyme and orange zest. Remove the pan from heat and let steep for 20 minutes. Strain.

Whisk the egg yolks and sugar together in a mixing bowl. Whisk in the infused milk. Return the custard to the saucepan and cook, stirring constantly, over medium heat until it thickens enough to lightly coat a spoon. Pour back into the bowl and chill.

71

$\mathscr{W}ine \ \mathscr{P}airing$

NETTLE–MUSSEL SOUP
CHATEAU STE. MICHELLE 2002 SAUVIGNON BLANC
HORSE HEAVEN VINEYARD

CARROT RAVIOLI
CHATEAU STE. MICHELLE & DR. LOOSEN 2003 EROICA RIESLING

SALMON
CHATEAU STE. MICHELLE 2002 CHARDONNAY
INDIAN WELLS VINEYARD

PUMPKIN BAY SOUFFLÉ
CHATEAU STE. MICHELLE 2000 LATE HARVEST SEMILLON

72

SAUVIGNON BLANC

COLUMBIA VALLEY

HORSE HEAVEN
VINEYARD

Chateau Ste Michelle

FOUNDED IN 1934, CHATEAU Ste. Michelle is the oldest winery in Washington State. The winery combines an ongoing dedication to research with a commitment to classic winemaking traditions. Known for its highly acclaimed Chardonnay, Riesling, Merlot and Cabernet, Chateau Ste. Michelle receives some of the highest accolades in the industry, including nine time winner of "Winery of the Year" honors from *Wine & Spirits* magazine.

Located fifteen miles northeast of Seattle, the winery is situated on eighty-seven wooded acres that were home to Seattle lumber baron Frederick Stimson in the early 1900s. Chateau Ste. Michelle owns thirty-four hundred acres of vineyards in the Columbia Valley in Eastern Washington, where conditions are ideal for growing ripe, flavorful grapes. Its best-known vineyards are Canoe Ridge Estate and Cold Creek.

During the summer, Chateau Ste. Michelle is home to the popular summer concert series where guests can enjoy picnics and wine on the Chateau's lawn while listening to top musical entertainment.

CHATEAU

STE. MICHELLE

STIMSON LANE VINEYARDS
& ESTATES,
OWNER

14111 NE 145TH

WOODINVILLE, WA 98072

425.415.3632

www.ste-michelle.com

PAN–SEARED WILD KING SALMON WITH SAUTÉED APPLES AND CIDER REDUCTION

SAFFRON MUSSEL BISQUE

BRAISED SONOMA DUCKLING WITH GRILLED ENDIVE AND SEASONAL FRUIT

LEMON SAGE FLAN

The Hunt Club

THE HUNT CLUB
IN THE SORRENTO HOTEL
BRIAN SCHEEHSER,
EXECUTIVE CHEF

900 MADISON
SEATTLE, WA 98104
206.343.6156
www.hotelsorrento.com

WALKING INTO THE HUNT CLUB IS LIKE STEPPING INTO TURN-OF-THE century—the previous century—elegance. Dark paneled walls, rich furnishings, and the quiet sophistication of being part of the famed Sorrento Hotel, set the scene for what's to come.

After you relax over cocktails, watching the flames dance in the fireplace, Executive Chef Brian Scheehser will tempt, then delight your palette with an opening course of Creamy Butternut Squash Ravioli or Fresh Pacific Northwest Salmon Bruschetta. For the second course, enjoy the Saffron Mussel Bisque or the Roasted Heirloom Tomato Rosemary Soup. Feel the comfort and the ambience of the room transport you to a relaxed state of well being as your entrées are placed before you—the fresh fish offering or the Pheasant Veronique or the lightly smoked Chargrilled Lamb Chops, served with a fine Kestrel Pinot Noir from the restaurant's extensive wine cellar.

This is a meal to be savored slowly, accompanied by good conversation and the time to enjoy it. Save room for *le piece d'resistance*—Profiteroles with Chocolate Sauce or Rainier Cherry Bread Pudding, a snifter of brandy, and the accompaniment of easy jazz on the piano.

If all that isn't enough, make the occasion even more special by having a Sorrento Hotel room key served up with your dessert. Afterall, a kiss at The Hunt Club in the Sorrento Hotel is voted the best place to kiss in Seattle.

Pan-Seared Wild King Salmon with Sautéed Apples and Cider Reduction

6 5 OZ PORTIONS WILD SALMON
BEURRÉ BLANC SAUCE
CHERVIL GARNISH
6 APPLES, PEELED,
CORED, AND SLICED THIN
SALT AND PEPPER TO TASTE
APPLE CIDER

❖ BEURRÉ BLANC
1 SMALL SHALLOT,
FINELY CHOPPED
2 OZ WHITE WINE
1 OZ LEMON JUICE
1 OZ HEAVY CREAM
8 OZ BUTTER
SALT AND PEPPER TO TASTE

SERVES 6

❖ Combine white wine and shallots. Reduce over medium heat by 2/3. Add in heavy cream and bring to a rolling boil. Remove from heat and whisk in butter and lemon juice. Season to taste.

Pan sear salmon until golden brown. (This may be done ahead of time and finished in the oven.) Reduce apple cider to the consistency of maple syrup. Sauté apples lightly in butter before serving. Garnish with butter sauce and chervil.

Place sautéed apples in the center of the plate. Top with seared salmon. Lightly drizzle sauce on top and garnish with chervil.

Saffron Mussel Bisque

SERVES 6

3 LBS PENN COVE MUSSELS
1 ONION, CHOPPED
1 LEEK, WHITE ONLY, CHOPPED
1 TBSP BUTTER
1 SPRIG SAVORY
1 TSP SAFFRON
2 QTS FISH STOCK (CLAM JUICE MAY BE SUBSTITUTED)
1 1/2 CUP WHITE WINE
2 LARGE RUSSET POTATOES, PEELED AND CHOPPED
1 QT HEAVY CREAM
SALT AND PEPPER TO TASTE
CHOPPED CHIVES TO GARNISH

Sweat onion, leek, and savory in butter. Add fish stock and saffron. Bring to a slow simmer.

Add mussels and steam until cooked, approximately 3 to 5 minutes. Remove mussels (reserve them for garnish) and all leeks. Onions and broth should be returned to the pot. Add remainder of ingredients. Simmer slowly until potatoes are completely cooked.

Cool slightly. Then blend very carefully. (This process should be done with extreme caution. Blender should be no more than half full. A towel over the top will aid in keeping the soup from splashing during this process.)

To serve, place 6 to 8 mussels in each bowl. Pour in hot bisque. Garnish with chopped chives.

Soup may be served immediately or cooled and reserved for later use.

Braised Sonoma Duckling with Grilled Endive and Seasonal Fruit

2 FULL BREASTS OF SONOMA DUCKLING

1 ORANGE, ZESTED

5 STEMS OREGANO, LEAVES ONLY

1 TSP OLIVE OIL

2 PIECES BELGIAN ENDIVE

2 WESTHAVEN PEACHES

4 BLACK MISSION FIGS

BLACK PEPPER

SALT

SERVES 4

Marinate breast of duckling with orange zest, olive oil, oregano, and light dusting of black pepper. Refrigerate for 6 to 8 hours to marry flavors.

Pan sear duck slowly, skin side down, to render fats and create a crisp skin. Flip duck and remove from heat. Let rest 5 minutes.

While resting, lightly grill endive and fruit to warm and develop flavors. Slice rested duck and serve with grilled endive and fruit. Add watercress garnish and light dusting of salt.

Lemon Sage Flan

SERVES 9

❖ Combine milk, cream, and sugar together. Over low heat, bring to a scald (just below the boiling point). Remove from heat. Add lemon juice and zest, plumped gelatin, and stir until dissolved. Pour into buttered molds* and refrigerate overnight. To unmold, briefly dip the molds in a hot water bath to loosen from the molds. Turn over onto serving plates.

❖ Cream butter and sugar together at medium speed in mixer until soft. Add finely chopped lemon and sage. Blend in flour and egg whites and mix until smooth, about 1 minute. Chill.

Cut a triangle shape in a plastic template. This will be the mold for your cookie. Turn a sheet pan upside down. Put a Sil-pat* baking sheet on top. Place template. Using an offset spatula, spread butter thin and evenly to fill the cutout. Remove template and bake at 350° for 5 to 7 minutes or until light golden brown. With a spatula, remove while warm, and form.

The forming process must be done while the cookie is hot. The cookie hardens as it cools. Glasses can be used to shape the cookie into an "S" shape.

❖ Take fresh sage leaves and dry in a 225° oven for 10 minutes, until dry. Lightly sprinkle with sugar and let stand for 5 minutes. Place in an airtight container. Add more sugar to cover.

❖ Combine sugar and water. Bring to a boil. Add lemon zest and cook for about 1 hour or until rind becomes transparent. Remove from syrup and place on a rack to dry, preferably overnight. Coat with sugar and place in airtight container. Reserve for presentation.

Flan molds and Sil-pat baking sheets are available at Sur la Table.

❖ LEMON FLAN

3 GELATIN SHEETS,
SOFTENED IN COLD WATER
27 OZ HEAVY CREAM
9 OZ WHOLE MILK
10 OZ SUGAR
3 LEMONS, ZESTED AND JUICED

❖ TUILLE BATTER

1 CUP SUGAR
4 EGG WHITES
6 OZ BUTTER, MELTED
1 CUP ALL-PURPOSE FLOUR
1 LEMON, ZESTED AND
CHOPPED FINE
9 FRESH SAGE LEAVES,
CHOPPED

❖ CANDIED SAGE LEAVES

FRESH SAGE LEAVES

79

❖ CANDIED LEMON PEEL

1 CUP SUGAR
1 CUP WATER
2 LEMONS, ZESTED WITH
A CHANNEL KNIFE

Wine Pairing

Pan-Seared Wild King Salmon with Sautéed Apples and Cider Reduction
1999 Yakima Valley Merlot

Saffron Mussel Bisque
2001 Old Vine Chardonnay

Braised Sonoma Duckling with Grilled Endive and Seasonal Fruit
2000 Signature Edition Syrah

Lemon Sage Flan
2002 37.5 Brix—A Very Late Harvest Merlot

KESTREL VINTNERS IS AN AWARD-winning winery with an attitude—a Washington State attitude. We simply refer to it as our Grand Cru Mentality. From our winery owners to our winemaker to our vineyard manager, the same unyielding commitment to absolute quality exists as it does in the Chateaux of the Haut-Medoc.

Flint Nelson, our winemaker, has over ten years of winemaking experience with Yakima Valley fruit. He handcrafts our grapes into wines with extraordinary fruit concentration and structure.

We opened our doors as a 3,000 case winery and are now at approximately 10,000 cases. Most of our production is in red varietals—Cabernet Sauvignon, Merlot, and Syrah. The remaining 10% is in Chardonnay and Viognier. Barrel aging plays an important part in our wine production. Our wines are aged one to two years in the finest French, American, and Hungarian oak barrels and allowed a minimum of two years bottle aging prior to release.

We start with the highest quality grapes from our renowned Kestrel View Estate Vineyard. We intentionally reduce our crop size by 40%-60% of Washington State norms and water stress our vines, producing small, highly flavored, intensely aromatic, and color-rich berries. These, in turn, produce Kestrel's award-winning wines.

KESTREL
VINTNERS

JOHN WALKER,
OWNER

2890 LEE ROAD

PROSSER, WA 99350

509.786.2675

www.kestrelwines.com

Walnut Fried Brie

icon Grill Braised Pear Salad

Potato Wrapped Halibut with Roasted Red Potatoes,

Sautéed Spinach, Lemon Butter and Balsamic Syrup

Texas Funeral Fudge Cake

icon Grill

icon GRILL
NICK MUSSER,
EXECUTIVE CHEF

1933 FIFTH AVENUE

SEATTLE, WA 98101

206.441.6330

www.icongrillseattle.com

FOR FASCINATING AND ECLECTIC ATMOSPHERE—PURE EYE-CANDY—
icon GRILL is the restaurant to visit. It's trademark glass art, sculpture, and elegant
yet quirky décor is only surpassed by its delightfully delectable food. "It's an over-the-
top rendition of a Victorian setting gone 21st century."(Frommers) The atmosphere
is casual, lively, and certain to impress locals as much as it does out-of-towners.

Once seated in a leather embossed booth and after checking out all there is to see,
it's time to get down to the business of dining.

How often can you find meatloaf wrapped in bacon, baked with a molasses glaze, and
served with mashed potatoes and gravy? How often do you remember parmesan
crusted sole that's so light and tasty, it stays on your mind long after you've eaten it?
How often do you choose to order mac and cheese at a restaurant simply because
you've never had better? Add a sophisticated repertoire of grilled salmon, steak,
chicken, lamb, pasta, pizza, and a slice of Texas Fudge Cake and you have a restaurant
with a menu as diverse as its art.

Walnut Fried Brie

1 SMALL WEDGE BRIE CHEESE
1 CUP WALNUTS, CHOPPED FINE
2 EGGS
1 TBSP MILK
1/2 CUP FLOUR
SALT AND PEPPER
3 CUPS VEGETABLE OIL FOR FRYING

❧ DRIED FRUIT CHUTNEY
1 CUP DRIED FRUIT
(A MIX OF CRANBERRIES, CHERRIES,
BLUEBERRIES, AND APRICOTS)
1 SHALLOT, PEELED AND
CHOPPED MEDIUM
1 CUP WATER
1/2 CUP DRY WHITE WINE
1/4 CUP SUGAR
2 TBSP WHOLE GRAIN MUSTARD
JUICE OF ONE LEMON
1 PEAR OR APPLE, PEELED AND DICED
1 TBSP OIL

SERVES 4

❧ Mix salt and pepper with the flour. Dust the Brie until completely coated. Knock off any excess flour. Mix eggs and milk in a small bowl. Dip Brie into the egg. Return to the flour and dredge again. Dip it back into the egg and then roll in the chopped walnuts, being sure to cover completely. Bring the cooking oil to 350° and carefully drop the Brie into the oil. Fry until golden brown. Drain and place directly onto a serving platter.

❧ Sauté the shallot in oil until soft in a small saucepan. Add all fruit, dried and fresh. Cook for 2 minutes. Deglaze with wine and add water, sugar and mustard. Simmer until fruit is soft and sauce is thick. Purée with immersion blender or in food processor until it resembles the consistency of thick jam. Add lemon juice and a touch of salt. Serve with fried Brie and fresh baguette.

84

icon Grill Braised Pear Salad

❧ PEARS
4 BOSC OR BARTLETT PEARS
4 TBSP BUTTER
1/2 CUP DRY WHITE WINE
1 TBSP PICKLING SPICE
2 TBSP SUGAR

❧ DRESSING
1/2 CUP RASPBERRY VINEGAR
1/4 CUP POMEGRANATE MOLASSES
1 SMALL SHALLOT, PEELED
1/2 EGG
1 1/2 CUPS OLIVE OIL
SALT AND PEPPER TO TASTE

SERVES 8 AS STARTERS OR 4 AS ENTREES

❧ Cut pears in half and core. Place flat side down into baking dish. Sprinkle all ingredients evenly over pears. Cover with a lid or foil and bake at 350° for 20 minutes or until pears are just tender. (Be careful. Riper pears will cook more quickly. Check after 10 minutes.) Let pears cool. Cut each half into 4 slices lengthwise and set aside.

❧ Place shallot, egg, vinegar, and molasses into a blender or food processor. Purée with two or three short bursts until mixed. While running, slowly drizzle in oil until emulsified. Season with salt and pepper, as desired.

✤ Melt butter and set aside. In a mixer or by hand, beat eggs and sugar until thick and creamy. Add all spices and slowly drizzle in butter until incorporated. In a bowl, mix pecans with butter/sugar mixture and coat the nuts evenly. Place the nuts on a cookie sheet and cook in a 300° oven for 20 minutes. Stir the nuts every 5 minutes, so they cook evenly. When golden brown, set aside to cool.

✤ Toss greens in a bowl with pears, dress as desired. Place salad evenly on 4 or 8 plates, arranging the pears on top. Sprinkle with blue cheese and pecans.

✤ PECANS

1 LB PECAN HALVES
4 TBSP BUTTER
1/3 LB BROWN SUGAR
1/2 EGG
2 TSP SALT
1 DASH CAYENNE PEPPER (OPTIONAL)
1 TBSP CHILI POWDER
1 TSP GROUND CUMIN
1/2 TSP GROUND PEPPER
1 TSP GROUND CORIANDER
1/2 TSP GROUND GINGER

✤ SALAD

1/2 LB MIXED BABY GREENS
1/4 LB OREGON BLUE CHEESE, CRUMBLED

85

Potato Wrapped Halibut with Roasted Red Potatoes, Sautéed Spinach, Lemon Butter and Balsamic Syrup

SERVES 4 ✤ ROASTED POTATOES

1 1/2 LB SMALL RED POTATOES
2 TBSP CORN OIL
1 TSP SALT
1 TSP GROUND BLACK PEPPER
1/4 TSP GRANULATED GARLIC

✤ Preheat the oven to 425°. Cut the potatoes in half and place them in a large saucepan of cold water. Bring the potatoes to a boil over high heat. Turn the heat down to medium and gently boil the potatoes until they are tender—15 to 20 minutes.

Drain the potatoes and place them in a large bowl. Add the corn oil and salt and pepper to the bowl and toss the potatoes to coat them well. Arrange the potatoes in a single layer on a shallow baking pan and roast in the oven until they are golden brown, about 15 minutes. Sprinkle with granulated garlic before serving.

✤ BALSAMIC SYRUP

2 CUPS BALSAMIC VINEGAR

✤ Place the vinegar in a small non-corrosive saucepan over high heat. Bring it to a boil. Reduce the heat to a slow boil. Reduce the vinegar until only a couple of tablespoons are left and it is thick and syrupy.

✤ LEMON BUTTER

2 TBSP SHALLOTS, MINCED
1/2 TSP CORN OIL
1/4 CUP DRY WHITE WINE
1/4 CUP CHAMPAGNE VINEGAR
1/4 CUP CREAM
1/2 LB UNSALTED BUTTER, SOFTENED
2 TSP LEMON JUICE
1/2 TSP SALT
1/4 TSP GROUND BLACK PEPPER

✤ In a small heavy saucepan over low heat, gently sauté the shallots in the corn oil for 2 minutes until they become transparent. Add the wine and Champagne vinegar. Turn up the heat and bring the mixture to a boil. Reduce the liquid by half. Add the cream and reduce by half again. Pass the reduction through a strainer to remove the shallots and return the liquid to the saucepan.

Bring the reduction to a slow boil. Divide the softened butter into 8 equal portions. Whisk the butter into the reduction, one portion at a time, until all the butter is incorporated. Remove the sauce from the heat. Season with the salt, pepper, and lemon juice.

✤ SAUTÉED SPINACH

4 BUNCHES FRESH SPINACH
2 TSP SHALLOTS, MINCED
1 1/2 TSP SALT
1/2 TSP GROUND BLACK PEPPER
1 TSP BUTTER

✤ Remove the stems from the spinach and wash the leaves well. Put a large pot of water on the stove and bring to a boil. Add the spinach to the boiling water. Cook for 2 minutes. Drain the spinach in a colander and refresh it with cold running water. Squeeze as much water as possible from the blanched spinach. Place the spinach in a large bowl and toss it well with the salt, pepper, and shallots.

Melt the butter in a sauté pan over medium high heat. Add the spinach and sauté until the spinach is hot, about 2 minutes.

✤ HALIBUT

4 6 OZ HALIBUT FILETS
1/4 TSP SALT
1/4 TSP GROUND BLACK PEPPER
1 VERY LARGE RUSSET POTATO
2 TBSP CORN OIL

✤ Preheat oven to 475°. Peel the potato and slice lengthwise very thinly. 8 slices are required for the dish. Season the halibut filets with salt and pepper. Wrap each filet in two slices of potato. Preheat a large non-stick sauté pan over medium high heat. Add the corn oil. Gently lay the wrapped halibut filets into the hot pan, seam side down. Cook the fish for 2 to 3 minutes until the bottom is golden brown. Turn the fish over and immediately put the pan into the oven for 3 to 5 minutes until the fish is cooked through and the bottom is brown.

Remove the potato-crusted halibut from the oven and serve with Oven Roasted Red Potatoes, Sautéed Spinach, and Lemon Butter Sauce. Drizzle with Balsamic Syrup just before serving.

Texas Funeral Fudge Cake

❖ Combine the sugar and evaporated milk in a large heavy sauce pot and place over medium high heat. Watch the pot carefully, and when the mixture comes to a boil, keep it boiling for exactly 9 minutes without stirring. Remove the pot from the heat and add the butter, chocolate, and vanilla. Stir the mixture until smooth. Transfer the mixture to a bowl and allow it to cool to room temperature. Cover the bowl with plastic wrap and chill in the refrigerator 3 hours or overnight.

❖ In the mixer, cream together the butter and sugars on high speed for 3 minutes. Scrape the bowl thoroughly. With the mixer running on medium speed, add the eggs 2 at a time, scraping down the bowl after each addition. Add vanilla. Mix thoroughly. Sift the flour, baking powder, and soda into a large bowl. Begin adding the dry ingredients and wet ingredients alternately in 3 additions. Start with the dry and finish with the wet. Scrape the bowl after each addition.

Divide the batter between 3 greased, floured, and parchment-lined cake pans. Bake the cakes in a preheated 350° oven for 30 to 35 minutes until a wooden pick inserted into the center of the layers comes out clean.

Cool the layers in the pans on wire racks for 10 minutes. Turn them out onto the racks until they cool completely.

ASSEMBLE CAKE

With a long serrated knife, cut the dome off each layer to make a flat surface. Then cut each layer in half. Place the fudge frosting into an electric mixer and beat with the paddle attachment on medium high speed until the frosting is soft, fluffy, and the color goes from a dark chocolate to a light milk chocolate color. Frost the cakes with frosting between each layer and frost a thick layer on the top. Frost the sides liberally. Let the cake set in the refrigerator for 1 hour before cutting.

❖ FUDGE FROSTING

2 CUPS GRANULATED SUGAR
2 CUPS EVAPORATED MILK
11 OZ UNSWEETENED CHOCOLATE, CHOPPED
1 CUP UNSALTED BUTTER, CHILLED, CUT INTO 1" PIECES
1 TSP VANILLA EXTRACT

❖ CAKE LAYERS

5 1/3 CUPS CAKE FLOUR
5 2/3 CUPS SUGAR
2 LB UNSALTED BUTTER
9 EGGS
2 TBSP BAKING POWDER
3 TSP BAKING SODA
1/2 TBSP SALT
2 2/3 CUPS COCOA POWDER
3 TSP VANILLA
2 2/3 CUP WATER
2 2/3 CUP WHOLE MILK

87

88

WALNUT FRIED BRIE
GEWÜRZTRAMINER

icon GRILL BRAISED PEAR SALAD
CHARDONNAY

POTATO WRAPPED HALIBUT WITH ROASTED RED POTATOES,
SAUTÉED SPINACH, LEMON BUTTER AND BALSAMIC SYRUP
MERLOT

TEXAS FUNERAL FUDGE CAKE
MUSCAT

CANOE RIDGE Vineyard — 2001 Merlot, Columbia Valley. Alc. 13.5% By Vol.

CANOE RIDGE
VINEYARD

CHALONE WINE GROUP,
OWNER

1102 W CHERRY STREET

WALLA WALLA, WA 99362

509.527.0885

www.canoeridgevineyard.com

AT CANOE RIDGE VINEYARD, WE GROW OUR GRAPES AT OUR UNIQUE ESTATE vineyard and use traditional French cellaring to produce an elegant, classic Merlot with the suppleness of Pinot Noir.

In 1982, Phil Woodward, cofounder of the Chalone Wine Group, tasted a Chardonnay that was said to be one of Washington's best. Impressed by the quality of the wine and intrigued by a winery that shared his last name—Woodward—he canceled his flight home, rented a car and set out to find the maker of that fine Chardonnay. The journey led him to the town of Lowden, home to Rick Small and Woodward Canyon Winery. This was the beginning of a friendship between the two men that eventually led to an introduction to a group of Washington farmers who, in 1989, started planting wine grapes on Canoe Ridge. A total of 143 acres are now in full production.

Our vineyard not only provides us with the fruit for our own wines, but a small amount is sold to two other wineries—Woodward Canyon Cabernet Sauvignon and The Hogue Cellars Cabernet Sauvignon.

Our estate vineyard overlooks the vast Umatilla National Wildlife Refuge, a popular nesting area for Great Basin Canada geese, several species of ducks, and other marsh and water birds.

In May 1995, we celebrated the release of the first wines from Canoe Ridge Vineyard and opened our Tasting Room where you can experience the best of Western Washington scenery while enjoying the best of Western Washington wines.

Pan Seared Veal Sweetbreads with Fennel and Port Caper Jus

Dungeness Crab Salad with Braeburn Apples and Red Radishes

Black Cod with Saffron Roasted Cauliflower, Spinach and Sorrel Mousse

Wild Huckleberry Bread Pudding with Ginger Ice Cream

Nell's

NELL'S RESTAURANT
PHILIP MIHALSKI,
OWNER

6804 GREENLAKE WAY N
SEATTLE, WA 98115
206.524.4044
www.nellsrestaurant.com

NELL'S OWNER PHILIP MIHALSKI WAS A FORMER CHEF AT MARCO'S SUPPER Club and Dahlia Lounge before setting off on his own to open Nell's. Named after his wife, Nell's comprises all the great characteristics of its former identity, Saleh al Lago—excellent food and a superbly professional wait staff. The atmosphere is classy while still allowing for a come-as-you-are clientele out to enjoy a delectable meal with friends. The warmth of the pale yellow walls is matched by the warmth of the host as he welcomes you to his culinary paradise.

Nell's seasonal menu promises favorites as well as the unusual. Dive into a plate of calamari with parsley salad and aioli before moving on to black truffle and leek risotto, so creamy it literally melts in your mouth. Enjoy an entrée of pan roasted duck with celery root purée and bing cherries or wild salmon with English peas, mint, and roasted shallot jus. Even as you finish, your palate is craving more.

Once a guest of Nell's, you will become a frequenter for the fine food, extensive wine cellar, and the impeccable service. And to complete your perfect evening—enjoy an after dinner stroll around beautiful Green Lake.

*Pan Seared
Veal Sweetbreads
with Fennel and
Port Caper Jus*

92

18 OZ VEAL SWEETBREADS
1 BULB FENNEL
1 TBSP SHALLOTS, FINELY CHOPPED
1/2 CUP CHICKEN STOCK
1/2 CUP VEAL STOCK
1/4 CUP PORT
1 TBSP CAPERS
FLOUR TO DREDGE SWEETBREADS
1 OZ OLIVE OIL
3 TBSP BUTTER
SALT AND PEPPER

SERVES 6

Soak sweetbreads overnight in water. Drain, trim off any excess fat or membrane. Cut into 6 3 oz pieces. Peel layers of fennel from core and cut into uniform julienne strips. Pick some green tops from the fennel and chop about 1 tbsp for garnish.

In a sauté pan, sweat shallots with 1 tbsp butter. Add chicken stock and fennel. Simmer for about 8 minutes until cooked. Season with salt and pepper.

Dry any excess water from the sweetbreads. Season with salt and pepper. Dredge in flour, shaking off any excess.

Heat oil in large sauté pan until smoking. Add sweetbreads. Cook 3 to 4 minutes per side until nicely browned all over and cooked through. Set aside. Deglaze pan with port. Add veal stock and reduce by half. Finish with capers, salt, pepper, and butter.

Reheat fennel. Add fronds and transfer to center of 6 plates. Place veal on top of fennel and spoon sauce around. Serve.

We fry parsnip pieces cut from the parsnip with a peeler and use this as a garnish.

Dungeness Crab Salad with
Braeburn Apples and Red Radishes

SERVES 4

Combine ingredients and season with salt and pepper to taste. Add additional lemon juice, if needed. Arrange salad in the center of 4 plates (pressing crab into a 3" ring mold makes an attractive plate). Dress greens for garnish with olive oil, salt and pepper. Arrange on top of crab. Serve.

8 OZ DUNGENESS CRAB, CLEANED
1/2 CUP APPLE, DICED SMALL
1/4 CUP RED RADISH, CUT JULIENNE
2 TBSP MAYONNAISE
1 1/2 TSP LEMON JUICE
1 TSP CHIVES, CHOPPED
SALT AND PEPPER

GARNISH
MIXED HERBS, FRISÉE, OR ANOTHER
GREEN OF YOUR CHOICE

Black Cod with Saffron Roasted Cauliflower, Spinach and Sorrel Mousse

6 6 OZ PIECES OF BLACK COD
WITH SKIN ON
1 SMALL HEAD OF CAULIFLOWER
12 OZ CLEANED SPINACH
2 OZ YOUNG SORREL
2 TSP SHALLOTS, FINELY CHOPPED
2 TBSP BUTTER
2 TBSP OLIVE OIL
3 OZ HEAVY CREAM
1/4 CUP WHITE WINE
1/4 CUP CHICKEN STOCK
1/4 TSP SAFFRON
SALT AND PEPPER

SERVES 6

Cut sorrel into julienne strips. Place in blender with 1 oz of cream and a pinch of salt. Blend until puréed. Whip rest of cream until stiff. Fold in sorrel purée. Add salt, if needed.

Cut the core out of the cauliflower. Slice into pieces about 1/4" thick. Bring wine to a boil and reduce by half. Add saffron and chicken stock. Bring back to a boil and simmer for about 5 minutes.

In a large sauté pan, add 1 tbsp of oil and heat over medium high. When hot, add cauliflower and salt and pepper. Cook, turning often, until lightly browned. Add saffron broth. Continue cooking until cauliflower is tender and liquid has reduced.

While cauliflower is cooking, heat a large sauté pan over high heat with 1 tbsp of oil. Season cod on both sides with salt and pepper. When pan is smoking hot, place cod in pan, skin side down. Cook about 4 minutes until skin is well browned. Turn fish and cook for 2 to 4 minutes more, depending upon thickness.

Heat 1 tbsp of butter with shallots. Add spinach to wilt. Season with salt and pepper. Add remaining 1 tbsp of butter to cauliflower. Check seasoning.

In 6 large flat bowls or plates, arrange cauliflower with saffron sauce on bottom. Divide spinach and place over the cauliflower on each plate. Place the cod on the spinach. Garnish with sorrel mousse. Serve.

94

Wild Huckleberry Bread Pudding with Ginger Ice Cream

SERVES 8 ❖

PUDDING

15 OZ OF BRIOCHE, CUT INTO 1" CUBES
7 EGG YOLKS
3 CUPS HALF AND HALF
1/2 CUP SUGAR
ZEST OF 1 LEMON
1/2 TSP SALT
3 TBSP CASSIS
2 CUPS HUCKLEBERRY

ICE CREAM

2 CUPS HALF AND HALF
1/2 CUP SUGAR
1 OZ PIECE OF GINGER, THINLY SLICED
6 EGG YOLKS

❖ Preheat oven to 350°.

Line a 9" cake pan bottom with parchment. Butter and flour sides.

Mix yolks, half and half, sugar, lemon zest, salt, and cassis together in a bowl. Add brioche and mix with a spatula. Let stand for 1 hour, mixing a couple of times. Add huckleberries and transfer to pan. Sprinkle top with 1 tbsp of sugar. Bake for about 1 hour or until top is lightly brown and center is set. Let cool and remove from pan.

❖ Combine ginger, half and half, and sugar in a heavy bottom, non-corrosive saucepan. Bring to a boil. Let steep for 15 minutes. Transfer some of the hot liquid into eggs and mix. Add mixture back into saucepan.

Over medium heat, stir constantly until mixture thickens and coats the back of a spoon. Remove from heat and pass custard through a fine strainer. Cool. Pour into ice cream machine and freeze.

Cut cake into 8 wedges, place a scoop of ice cream on top and serve. You can garnish with a few extra huckleberries or make a sauce with huckleberries.

Wine Pairing

Pan Seared Veal Sweetbreads with Fennel
and Port Caper Jus
2003 Sauvignon Blanc

Dungeness Crab Salad with Braeburn Apples
and Red Radishes
2001 Sogno (Cabernet Franc)

Black Cod with Saffron Roasted Cauliflower,
Spinach and Sorrel Mousse
2001 Merlot

Wild Huckleberry Bread Pudding with
Ginger Ice Cream
2002 Sweet Catherine

2001

MERLOT

TRADITIONALLY PRODUCED BORDEAUX STYLE WINE

COLUMBIA VALLEY

PRODUCED AND BOTTLED BY
DISTEFANO WINERY, LTD. WOODINVILLE, WA.

750 ML   ALC. 14.6% BY VOL

MARK NEWTON, FOUNDER, OWNER, and winemaker of DiStefano Winery, is dedicated to producing small lot, Bordeaux-style wines of the highest quality. The winery uses traditional methods and applies gravity flow techniques for the gentle handling of the grapes.

DISTEFANO
WINERY

MARK NEWTON,
OWNER

12280 WOODINVILLE DRIVE NE

WOODINVILE, WA 98072

425.487.1648

www.distefanowinery.com

The wines from DiStefano have consistently received excellent marks from the national wine press for high quality handmade wines made from varietals that are demonstrating exceptional performance in the vineyards of the Columbia Valley.

DiStefano wines were a gift to Newton's wife Donna in tribute to her family, who combine great personal and business integrity with a strong sense of tradition. In keeping with this family tradition, DiStefano Winery dedicates its wines to those who enjoy them and to those who create them—the growers in the field, the cellar workers, and DiStefano's support staff.

Singing Pink Scallops "In Purgatory"

Truffled Oyster and Autumn Vegetable Soup

Braised Alaskan Halibut Cheeks Grenobloise with Herb Salad and Pine Nut Gremolata

Warm Huckleberry Buckle

The Oceanaire

THE OCEANAIRE
SEAFOOD ROOM
KEVIN DAVIS,
EXECUTIVE CHEF

1700 SEVENTH AVENUE
SEATTLE, WA 98101
206.267.2277
www.theoceanaire.com

THE OCEANAIRE SEAFOOD ROOM IS BEAUTIFUL, SLEEK, AND VERY RETRO. It's as though a 1930's or 1940's luxury cruise liner glided gracefully into the middle of downtown Seattle.

With "Ultra-Fresh" fish flown in daily, The Oceanaire offers salmon as well as imaginative preparations of blue marlin (the fish that graces The Oceanaire's elegant logo), red snapper, mahi-mahi, swordfish, Dover sole, and the truly exceptional Sea of Cortez bluefin tuna. The fresh oyster bar is the ultimate spot for martinis and a wide selection of oysters on the half shell. Or travel back to another culinary era by enjoying Oysters Rockerfeller and Baked Alaska while listening to the background sounds of Louis Armstrong or Glenn Miller.

The service is exceptional. The wait staff at The Oceanaire is just as attentive to the diner who orders the fish and chips as it is to the diner who feasts on the live Maine lobster.

Named one of America's Best Restaurants by *Bon Appétit*, The Oceanaire has landed in *Gourmet's Guide to America's Best Restaurants* and was voted "Best Newcomer" by *Seattle Magazine*. Chef Kevin Davis was also voted *Seattle Magazine's* "Chef To Watch."

Singing Pink Scallops "In Purgatory"

40 PIECES SINGING PINK SCALLOPS
OR LITTLENECK CLAMS, ABOUT
THE SIZE OF A SILVER DOLLAR.
RINSE WELL TO REMOVE ALL GRIT
1 CUP ANDOUILLE SAUSAGE, SLICED
(OR SUBSTITUTE ANOTHER SPICY
SAUSAGE SUCH AS CHORIZO)
2 OZ OLIVE OIL
1/2 CUP WHITE WINE
1 CUP TOMATOES, DICED
2 TBSP GARLIC, SLICED
1 CUP FRESH BASIL
2 TBSP SERRANO CHILI, SLICED
2 TBSP WHOLE BUTTER
2 TBSP ORANGE ZEST
1 TSP TABASCO
SALT AND FRESHLY GROUND
BLACK PEPPER TO TASTE

SERVES 4

Preheat large sauté pan over medium high heat (pan #1). Place clams, tomatoes, white wine, butter, and salt and pepper in another sauté pan of equal size (pan #2). Add olive oil to pan #1 and proceed to sauté sausage until evenly brown. Add garlic and render until garlic starts to turn slightly brown. Add basil and cook until basil begins to crisp. Add Serrano chilis and orange zest.

Remove from heat and invert pan #2 onto pan #1 and quickly return to heat. Cook for 5 minutes and lift pan #1. One by one, transfer scallops as they open to a large serving bowl. When all scallops are open and transferred, adjust seasoning and pour over clams. Serve with crusty French bread and a nice Riesling.

100

Truffled Oyster and Autumn Vegetable Soup

2 OZ BUTTER
1 1/2 OZ FLOUR
2 OZ ONION, 1/4" DICE
2 OZ CELERY, 1/4" DICE
1 1/2 OZ CARROTS, 1/4" DICE
1 1/2 OZ BUTTERNUT SQUASH, 1/4" DICE
1 1/2 OZ LEEKS, 1/4" DICE
2 OZ CHANTERELLE MUSHROOMS (OR
SUBSTITUTE OYSTER MUSHROOMS)
1/2 OZ GARLIC, FINELY CHOPPED
1/2 TBSP THYME
1/2 TBSP PARSLEY
1/2 TBSP GREEN ONION
4 CUPS MILK
7 TSP SALT
1 TSP WHITE PEPPER
1/2 TBSP TABASCO
1/2 TBSP BUTTER
1 1/2 CUP OYSTERS
1 TBSP TRUFFLE OIL

SERVES 4

In a heavy gauge, non-reactive saucepan, add butter and garlic and melt over medium heat until garlic is blonde. Add carrots, onions, leeks, celery, and mushrooms. Sauté until onions are translucent, being careful not to brown. When vegetables are tender, add salt, pepper, thyme, and green onions. Add flour and lower heat. Cook until flour is completely incorporated. Add half of the milk and bring to a boil, stirring constantly until smooth and silky. Add remaining milk. Continue to cook, stirring constantly, until flavors begin to meld and a soup-like consistency is achieved. Add oysters and remaining ingredients. Simmer for 10 minutes.

Serve.

Braised Alaskan Halibut Cheeks Grenobloise
with Herb Salad and Pine Nut Gremolata

SERVES 4

✤ Preheat oven to 450°. Preheat olive oil in a heavy gauge braising pan over medium high heat. Season halibut cheeks with salt and pepper and toss in Wondra flour. Brown halibut cheeks in oil. Remove from braising skillet. Add 1 oz of butter to sauté pan and brown. Add shallots and render until tender. Deglaze with lemon juice and reduce by half. Add chicken stock and bring to boil.

Add halibut cheeks and return to boil. Remove from heat and place in oven. Cook for 8 minutes or until cheeks are tender. Turn off oven. Place cheeks on serving platter and return sauce to flame. Add zest, sections, capers, and remaining butter. Season with salt and pepper. Remove from heat.

Place serving platter in oven to warm. When cheeks are warm, garnish with croutons, then the sauce, and finally gremolata and herb salad. Serve immediately with lemon whipped potatoes.

✤ Preheat Teflon skillet on medium-high heat. Sprinkle a fine but even layer of parmesan cheese into the bottom of skillet. Cook until cheese begins to brown. Gently lift an edge of the cheese and the mass should come up like a crêpe. Flip it over and cook briefly until brown on the other side. Remove from pan and allow to cool. Crush coarsely with pine nuts. Keep in a dry place until needed

✤ **BRAISED HALIBUT CHEEKS**

2 LBS HALIBUT CHEEKS, EVEN IN SIZE, PREFERABLY 2" IN DIAMETER
1 CUP WONDRA FLOUR
2 CUPS CHICKEN STOCK
4 TBSP SHALLOTS, FINELY DICED
4 LEMONS, 2 ZESTED, 2 SECTIONED, JUICE RESERVED
1 1/2 TBSP CAPERS, DRAINED
1 CUP WHITE BREAD, 1/2" DICED CROUTONS, TOASTED IN BUTTER
2 OZ WHOLE BUTTER
4 OZ EXTRA VIRGIN OLIVE OIL
1/2 CUP HERB SALAD (25% BASIL LEAVES, 25% CHIVES, 25% FLAT LEAF PARSLEY, 25% TARRAGON)
SALT AND FRESHLY GROUND BLACK PEPPER

✤ GREMOLATA
1/4 CUP PINE NUTS, FRESHLY TOASTED
1/4 CUP PARMESAN CHEESE
1 12" TEFLON SKILLET

101

102

Warm Huckleberry Buckle

SERVES 4

✤ In a stainless steel mixing bowl, add huckleberries, flour, and cornstarch. Mix well.

✤ Mix flour, salt, and sugar well. Add diced butter and cut into flour with pastry cutter until butter is pea-sized. Add ice water and mix gently by hand. Refrigerate for 20 minutes before rolling out.

✤ In a stainless steel mixing bowl, add flour, sugar, oats, cinnamon, and vanilla. Mix well. Add butter. Cut butter into flour with a pastry cutter until mixture resembles small peas.

ASSEMBLING THE BUCKLE

Preheat oven to 350°. Spray 4 individual 8 oz soup cups with non-stick spray. Roll pie dough out to 1/8" thickness. Cut into 4 separate 6" circles. Place in 4 individual 8 oz soup cups. Divide huckleberry filling among the 4 cups. Cover with crumble topping. Pull dough up around sides. Bake in oven for 45 minutes or until golden brown (internal temperature is 175°).

Remove from oven. Serve warm with a scoop of vanilla ice cream.

✤ FILLING

1 LB FRESH HUCKLEBERRIES, FROZEN IF FRESH ARE NOT AVAILABLE

1 CUP SUGAR

2 TBSP FLOUR

1 TBSP CORNSTARCH

✤ PIE DOUGH

3 CUPS ALL PURPOSE FLOUR

2 CUPS BUTTER

1 CUP ICE WATER

2 TBSP SUGAR

1/4 TSP SALT

✤ CRUMBLE TOPPING

3 OZ FLOUR

2 OZ OATS

2 OZ SUGAR

2 OZ BROWN SUGAR

1/4 LB UNSALTED BUTTER, DICED

1/4 TSP CINNAMON

1/4 TSP VANILLA

103

Wine Pairing

SINGING PINK SCALLOPS "IN PURGATORY"
2002 WOODWARD CANYON DRY RIESLING

TRUFFLED OYSTER AND AUTUMN VEGETABLE SOUP
2002 WOODWARD CANYON COLUMBIA VALLEY CHARDONNAY

BRAISED ALASKAN HALIBUT CHEEKS GRENOBLOISE
WITH HERB SALAD AND PINE NUT GREMOLATA
2001 WOODWARD CANYON COLUMBIA VALLEY SYRAH

104

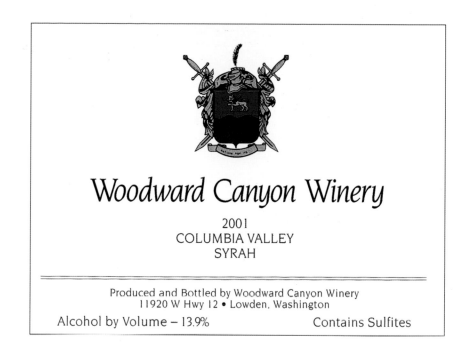

Woodward Canyon Winery

2001
COLUMBIA VALLEY
SYRAH

Produced and Bottled by Woodward Canyon Winery
11920 W Hwy 12 • Lowden, Washington

Alcohol by Volume – 13.9%   Contains Sulfites

WOODWARD
CANYON WINERY

RICK SMALL AND
DARCEY FUGMAN-SMALL,
OWNERS

11920 W HIGHWAY 12
LOWDEN, WA 99360
509.525.4129
www.woodwardcanyon.com

RICK SMALL AND HIS WIFE, DARCEY FUGMAN-SMALL, ESTABLISHED Woodward Canyon Winery in 1981. The winery was named for the canyon Rick's family farmed and where the Estate Vineyard is now located.

Rick planted the first of forty-six acres of the Woodward Canyon Estate Vineyard in 1976 on his family's dryland wheat ranch. Woodward Canyon produces premium award-winning wines including Cabernet Sauvignon, Merlot, Cabernet Franc, Sauvignon Blanc, Chardonnay, and Barbera. The winery also purchases grapes from selected growers and is a partner in Champoux Vineyard.

Since the beginning, Rick determined that quality would take precedence over quantity. Consequently, Woodward Canyon has remained small, increasing its production from 1,200 cases in 1981 to approximately 13,000 cases in 2003. In 2003, Kevin Mott joined Woodward Canyon as Winemaker, with Rick moving to Director of Production to focus his attention on vineyard quality.

Woodward Canyon also offers its Nelms Road label Merlot and Cabernet Sauvignon made from Walla Walla Valley and Washington State grapes. Nelms Road was developed to produce delicious and affordable red wine from young vineyards or declassified Woodward Canyon wine production.

Located in the community of Lowden in Washington's Walla Walla Valley, Woodward Canyon invites guests to enjoy their wines in their tasting room, a restored 1870's farmhouse.

Roasted Beet and Herbed Goat Cheese Napoleon

Butternut Squash Chowder with Dungeness Crab

Curried Braised Lamb Shanks

Bittersweet Chocolate Macadamia Nut Torte

Ovio Bistro

OVIO BISTRO
SHING AND ELLIE CHIN,
OWNERS
EDDIE MONTOYA,
EXECUTIVE CHEF

3247 CALIFORNIA AVENUE SW
SEATTLE, WA 98116
206.935.1774
www.oviobistro.com

IN THIS BUSY WEST SEATTLE NEIGHBORHOOD, YOU'LL FIND A RESTAURANT jewel - one of those little secrets you want to keep to yourself but can't bear to. Ovio Bistro Eclectica shines bright, reflecting its name with an imaginative, eclectic menu nestled comfortably in its intimate space.

Owners Shing and Ellie Chin opened Ovio Bistro in the fall of 2002 after careers in some of the best houses in Seattle. They invented the name as a play on the French word meaning egg. Eggs symbolize new life and, with their second child on the way and a restaurant about to open, the Chins were all about new beginnings.

With a cast of seasoned veterans (all former co-workers), the service is hard to beat. Rave reviews and being chosen "Best New Restaurant 2003" by *Seattle Magazine* have made Ovio Bistro a favorite dining destination for patrons from all areas of Seattle.

Ovio features flavors of the world, created with the best in Northwest ingredients. Each dish is artfully and passionately created by twenty-five-year-old "wunderkind" Chef Eddie Montoya. The carefully selected wine list features familiar and little known wineries, all chosen to perfectly complement the menu and ensure you of an evening of palate-pleasing fun.

Roasted Beet and Herbed Goat Cheese Napoleon

3 LARGE RED BEETS, ROASTED, PEELED
AND CHOPPED IN 1/4" DICES
2 LARGE GOLDEN BEETS, ROASTED,
PEELED AND CHOPPED IN 1/4" DICES
1/2 CUP OLIVE OIL
SALT AND PEPPER TO TASTE
RECIPE FOR HERBED GOAT CHEESE
RECIPE FOR APPLE FENNEL SLAW

❖ HERBED GOAT CHEESE
1 LB GOAT CHEESE
2 TBSP TARRAGON, CHOPPED
1 TBSP GARLIC, MINCED
2 TSP FRESHLY GROUND PEPPER

❖ APPLE FENNEL SLAW
2 MEDIUM JONIGOLD APPLES
1 LARGE FENNEL BULB, WHITE PART ONLY
JUICE OF ONE LEMON
2 TBSP OLIVE OIL
SALT AND PEPPER TO TASTE

SERVES 4

Mix roasted red beets in a small bowl with 1/4 cup olive oil and salt and pepper. In a separate bowl, mix roasted golden beets with remainder of olive oil and season with salt and pepper. Set aside.

❖   Combine all ingredients in small bowl and mix well. Set aside until needed.

❖   Julienne apple and fennel into thin pieces. In a bowl, combine the lemon juice, olive oil, and salt and pepper. Mix in apple and fennel. Set aside.

TO ASSEMBLE THE NAPOLEON

Line the insides of small, 6 oz ramekins with plastic wrap. Add enough red beets to cover the bottom of the ramekin. Press gently to set beets into place. Add 2 tsp of Herbed Goat Cheese on top of red beets and smooth out over beets until even. Press 2 1/2 tbsp of golden beets on top of goat cheese. Place in another layer of goat cheese. Finish with a layer of red beets.

When done layering, gently press on top of Napolean to set in ramekin. Using a plate on top of the ramekin, gently turn ramekin over onto plate to release Napolean. Carefully lift off plastic wrap. Repeat with remaining Napoleans. Add a small pouf of Apple Fennel Slaw to the top of each napolean. Serve immediately.

108

Butternut Squash Chowder with Dungeness Crab

SERVES 4-6

In a large pot, sauté the bacon over medium high heat until cooked but not crispy, about 8 minutes. Without draining the bacon, add the butter to the pot and let melt. Add onions, carrots, celery, ginger, garlic, and lemongrass and sauté for 10 minutes. Add the butternut squash, wine, clam juice, heavy cream, and coconut milk. Bring to a boil and then reduce heat to low and let simmer for about 30 minutes. Season with salt and white pepper and add fresh herbs. Remove lemongrass stalks.

Ladle into bowls and top with fresh Dungeness crab.

1/2 LB BACON, DICED
1/2 LB BUTTER
2 MEDIUM ONIONS, CHOPPED
2 MEDIUM CARROTS, CHOPPED
3 STALKS CELERY, CHOPPED
4 TBSP GINGER, MINCED
3 TBSP GARLIC, MINCED
2 STALKS LEMONGRASS
1 LARGE BUTTERNUT SQUASH, CHOPPED
2 CUPS WHITE WINE
2 CUPS CLAM JUICE
2 CUPS HEAVY CREAM
3 CUPS COCONUT MILK
4 TBSP FRESH THYME
4 TBSP FRESH CILANTRO
SALT AND WHITE PEPPER TO TASTE
1 LB FRESH DUNGENESS CRAB MEAT

109

Curried Braised Lamb Shanks

6 LAMB SHANKS
1/4 CUP FENNEL SEED
1/2 CUP CORIANDER SEED
3 CUPS FLOUR
1 CUP CURRY POWDER
6 TBSP CANOLA OIL
1 BOTTLE RED WINE
1 1/2 CUPS LIGHT SOY SAUCE
2 LARGE ONIONS, CHOPPED
2 CELERY STALKS, CHOPPED
3 CARROTS, CHOPPED
1/2 CUP GINGER, MINCED
1/2 CUP GARLIC, MINCED
4 JALAPEÑO PEPPERS, SEEDED
AND CHOPPED
2 TBSP DRIED THYME
6 LIME LEAVES OR
2 WHOLE QUARTERED LIMES
SALT AND PEPPER

SERVES 6

Season shanks with salt and pepper. Grind fennel and coriander seeds in a spice grinder or clean coffee grinder. Combine with the flour and curry powder in a large bowl. Dredge shanks, one at a time, through flour mixture.

In a Dutch oven over high heat, add the canola oil. When oil is hot, add the shanks and brown on all sides, about 8 minutes. When all shanks are browned, add red wine and soy sauce to deglaze the bottom of the pan. Let simmer for 10 minutes. Add onions, celery, carrots, ginger, garlic, jalapeños, thyme, and lime leaves.

Cover pot and simmer for 3 to 4 hours until meat begins to fall off of the bone. Remove the shanks to a serving platter and keep warm. Reduce liquid over medium heat until it thickens slightly, about 10 minutes. Remove lime leaves or lime pieces and purée sauce with a hand blender until smooth. Taste and add salt and pepper, if needed.

Serve lamb shanks over saffron couscous with roasted root vegetables, such as carrots and turnips. Spoon sauce over top of shanks and vegetables. Serve.

110

Bittersweet Chocolate Macadamia Nut Torte

SERVES 6-8

❧ Preheat oven to 350°. Butter and flour a 10" spring form pan.

Melt butter in sauce pan over medium heat. Remove from heat. Add chocolate. Whisk chocolate into butter until chocolate melts. Add sugar and incorporate into chocolate mixture. Whisk eggs in, one at a time. At this point, mixture may look grainy, but continue to whisk until smooth. Add liqueur. Mix in flour and salt. Gently stir in 2 cups of macadamia nuts, reserving the rest of the nuts for garnish.

Pour chocolate mixture into prepared pan and bake in preheated oven for approximately 1 hour. Top will puff up and crack slightly. Check for doneness by inserting knife in center of torte. If knife comes out clean, torte is done. Let cool. Remove from pan by running a knife along the inside of the pan to loosen the torte.

❧ To glaze torte, bring cream to a simmer in a medium saucepan. Remove from heat and add chocolate. Whisk until melted and smooth. Whisk in liqueur. Let glaze sit for a minute to thicken, whisking occasionally. When glaze is thicker but still pourable, drizzle 1 1/2 cups over the top of the torte and spread along the sides of the torte with a knife or icing spatula. Spread remaining glaze over top of torte, smoothing it out as you go. Sprinkle remaining macadamia nuts on top of torte and then freeze torte for about 8 minutes to set glaze. Let stand at room temperature before slicing and serving. Serve with whipped cream and fresh berries.

❧ TORTE

2 STICKS UNSALTED BUTTER, CUT INTO PIECES
12 OUNCES BITTERSWEET CHOCOLATE, CHOPPED
1 1/2 CUPS SUGAR
6 LARGE EGGS
1/3 CUP CHAMBORD (OR OTHER RASPBERRY LIQUEUR)
2/3 CUP FLOUR
1/2 TSP SALT
2 1/2 CUPS MACADAMIA NUTS, CHOPPED

❧ GLAZE

1 CUP HEAVY CREAM
10 OZ BITTERSWEET CHOCOLATE
1/4 CUP CHAMBORD (OR OTHER RASPBERRY LIQUEUR)

111

Wine Pairing

112

ROASTED BEET AND HERBED GOAT CHEESE NAPOLEON
SHIRLEY MAYS SEMILLON
WALLA WALLA VALLEY APPELLATION

BUTTERNUT SQUASH CHOWDER
WITH DUNGENESS CRAB
DUNHAM CELLARS CABERNET SAUVIGNON
COLUMBIA VALLEY

CURRIED BRAISED LAMB SHANKS
DUNHAM CELLARS SYRAH
COLUMBIA VALLEY

BITTERSWEET CHOCOLATE MACADAMIA NUT TORTE
DUNHAM CELLARS SEMILLON ICE WINE
RED MOUNTAIN

USING GRAPES FROM SOME of the finest vineyards in the Walla Walla, Yakima, and Columbia valleys, Dunham Cellars has established an award-winning reputation for Cabernet Sauvignon and Syrah. When winemaker Eric Dunham's first vintage was released, a 1995 Cabernet Sauvignon, *Wine Enthusiast Magazine* deemed it one of the finest wines made in Washington. Dunham Cellars' Syrah is also earning high marks with wine writers and consumers. Each wine label features Eric's creative artistry with its hand-painted artist series design.

The winery makes its home in a rustic remodeled World War II airplane hangar in Walla Walla. The Walla Walla Valley has become a true destination getaway for wine lovers across the world. There isn't a better time to visit the Valley than on one of the three Open House weekends held every year. At Dunham Cellars, we make sure your experience during these weekends is memorable. You'll meet the winemakers, drink wonderful wines, and feast on exquisite hors d'oeuvres as music and the scent of the Valley's flowers fill the air.

DUNHAM
CELLARS

MIKE AND JOANNE DUNHAM,
ERIC DUNHAM,
OWNERS

150 E BOEING AVENUE
WALLA WALLA, WA 99362
509.529.4685
www.dunhamcellars.com

DUNGENESS CRAB COCKTAIL

ARUGULA SALAD WITH OLYMPIA OYSTER CROUTONS

THAI CURRY PENNE

MOLTEN CHOCOLATE CAKE

Ponti

PONTI SEAFOOD GRILL
RICHARD MALIA,
OWNER

3014 THIRD AVENUE N
SEATTLE, WA 98109
206.284.3000
www.PontiSeafoodGrill.com

HOW DOES AHI TUNA START SPEAKING TO THE PALATE IN ITALIAN AS Carpaccio? Where does the fragrant and delectable fusion of Occident meets Orient in Thai Curry Penne Pasta with Dungeness Crab fit in this equation? These culinary delights began as brainchildren of Seattle restaurateur and culinary Marco Polo, Richard Malia, and his wife Sharon.

In 1990, Richard created a modern mosaic. He combined his intimate knowledge of Northwest bounty, the classical culinary techniques of Europe, and the palate-pleasing flavors, scents, and spices of Asia to create Ponti Seafood Grill. Built to spec from the imagination of Richard Malia, Ponti is styled after a Mediterranean villa. Located on Seattle's Ship Canal, each of Ponti's three dining rooms and two outdoor patios have showcase vistas of the water and the Fremont and Aurora bridges.

Lauded in the *Zagat Guide* as "a gorgeous spot at the south side of the Fremont Bridge. A serene, elegant seafooder with a well-deserved reputation," Ponti is known as Seattle's finest for its Northwest seafood and Pacific Rim "fusion" cuisine. Ponti's extensive wine list has received *Wine Spectator* awards of excellence for thirteen years running. Rave reviews from local and national press and honors such as *Seattle Magazine's* "Best Seafood Restaurant" and "Best of the Northwest" as well as *Gourmet Magazine's* "Top Table" have remained de rigueur for Ponti.

These days at Ponti find Richard handpicking grape leaves from the lovely mature arbor at the restaurant, wrapping them around halibut, and pairing them on the plate with cous cous to be enjoyed as an afternoon entrée. The sights, scents, and flavors of Ponti continue to surprise and delight. The culinary journey continues!

Dungeness Crab Cocktail

3 OZ DUNGENESS CRAB
2 OZ RIPE MANGO, DICED
2 SLICES RIPE MANGO
1 TBSP ITALIAN PARSLEY
CHIFFONADE

SERVES 4

✤ Add tangerine zest and juice, and egg yolk to food processor and process slowly. Add 1 cup of Canola oil until emulsified. Add salt and pepper to taste.

✤ AIOLI

ZEST AND JUICE OF 2 TANGERINES
1 EGG YOLK
1 CUP CANOLA OIL
SALT AND PEPPER TO TASTE

✤ In strainer, blanch chives in boiling water for 10 seconds. From hot water, plunge into ice water. When cold, squeeze out excess water. Chop finely, then add to a blender with 1 cup of Canola oil. Strain through a coffee filter until clear.

✤ CHIVE OIL

1 CUP CANOLA OIL
1 BUNCH CHIVES

ASSEMBLY

Toss crab with parsley and enough aioli to coat. In 3" diameter ring mold, place half of the crab. Place diced mango on top of crab. Top with remainder of the crab. Garnish with mango slices. Drizzle plate with olive oil. Garnish top with parsley sprig.

Arugula Salad with Olympia Oyster Croutons

✤ OYSTER CROUTONS

20 OLYMPIA OYSTERS
4 CUPS PANKO ASIAN STYLE
BREADCRUMBS
1 TBSP CAYENNE

SERVES 4

✤ To make the oyster croutons, toss the panko with the cayenne and pat the oysters dry. Lightly coat the oysters in the panko and place in a hot dry skillet until lightly toasted.

116

❖ Wash and dry the salad greens. Gently toss with the vinegar and oil. Season the greens with salt and pepper. Shave the manchego over the greens. Place the oyster croutons on top.

2 OZ ARUGULA

4 OZ MANCHEGO CHEESE

4 TBSP WHITE BALSAMIC VINEGAR

6 TBSP EXTRA VIRGIN OLIVE OIL

SALT AND PEPPER TO TASTE

Thai Curry Penne

SERVES 4

❖ TOMATO CHUTNEY

1/2 CUP RICE VINEGAR

1 TSP GRATED GINGER

1/4 CUP BROWN SUGAR

2 TSP LEMON JUICE

1 16 OZ CAN PEAR TOMATOES, DRAINED AND CHOPPED

1 STICK OF CINNAMON

❖ Combine the vinegar, ginger, brown sugar, and lemon juice. Simmer 5 minutes. Add the tomatoes and cinnamon. Simmer 30 minutes. Remove from heat and set aside.

❖ In a large saucepan, combine the butter, garlic, onion, apple, curry, and salt and pepper. Sauté over high heat until onions are soft.

❖ CURRY

1 TBSP BUTTER

1 TSP GARLIC, CHOPPED

1/4 CUP ONION, DICED

1 LARGE GRANNY SMITH APPLE, CORED AND DICED

2 TSP CURRY POWDER

1/4 TSP SALT AND PEPPER

1 CUP MARSALA WINE

1 CUP CHICKEN BROTH

3 TSP THAI RED-CURRY PASTE

2 TSP THAI FISH SAUCE

1 CUP COCONUT MILK

1 CUP WHIPPING CREAM

1/2 LB PENNE PASTA, COOKED ACCORDING TO PACKAGE DIRECTIONS

1/4 LB CRABMEAT

CHOPPED FRESH BASIL

Add Marsala to the apple/onion mixture and reduce by half. Add the chicken broth, curry paste, and fish sauces. Simmer 10 minutes. Let cool and blend pureé in a food processor or blender. Transfer back to the saucepan and add the coconut milk and cream. Cool until thickened, about 10 to 15 minutes.

117

Drain the pasta and combine with the crabmeat and sauce. Divide between plates and top with the tomato chutney and fresh basil.

Note: There is enough sauce in this recipe for 3/4 to 1 lb of pasta.

118

Molten Chocolate Cake

SERVES 6

8 OZ SCHOKINAG CHOCOLATE PISTOLES
(64% OR HIGHER)

In a double boiler, melt the chocolate and butter. Add the sugar and
1 1/2 tsp of water.

8 OZ BUTTER

4 OZ SUGAR

2 1/2 OZ FLOUR

In another bowl, beat the eggs and the flour until smooth. Combine
the chocolate mixture into the egg mixture. Pour 4 oz into buttered
baking dishes. Cook at 500° for 4 to 6 minutes. Remove from oven
when just barely set. Run a knife around the inside of the baking dish to
release the cake from the pan. Place an inverted plate over the dish, then
flip the cake and plate over to serve. Garnish with whipped cream and
seasonal berries.

5 EGGS

119

Wine Pairing

DUNGENESS CRAB COCKTAIL
2003 SAUVIGNON BLANC

ARUGULA SALAD WITH OLYMPIA OYSTER CROUTONS
2003 SANGIOVESE ROSÉ

THAI CURRY PENNE
2003 VIOGNIER

MOLTEN CHOCOLATE CAKE
2001 CABERNET SAUVIGNON

LOCATED IN WASHINGTON STATE'S LOVELY WALLA WALLA VALLEY, Waterbrook Winery was founded in 1984 by Eric and Janet Rindal. Our name was chosen to complement the translation from Nez Perce Indian dialect for the name Walla Walla, meaning "running water." Waterbrook Chardonnay is now recognized as one of the most consistent, best values in its very competitive field.

With every vintage, knowledge of individual vineyard characteristics and winemaking subtleties has contributed to Waterbrook wines' complexity and flavor profiles. The goal for the red wines has been to make softer, fleshier wines for early enjoyment while still maintaining the wines' depth and structure. Results have been gratifying and the demand for both the Cabernet Sauvignon and Merlot has been far beyond supply. Waterbrook Chardonnay is now recognized as one of the most consistent, best values in its field.

For five years, *Wine Spectator* has listed it as one of the world's top fifty wine values. Every year, new French, American, and European oak is added and the careful work of barrel fermentation continues—a Waterbrook tradition for Chardonnay.

WATERBROOK WINERY

ERIC RINDAL, OWNER

31 E MAIN

WALLA WALLA, WA 99362

509.522.1262

www.waterbrook.com

Scrambled Egg with Crème Fraîche and White Sturgeon Caviar

Cured Troll King Salmon with a Parsley Root–Chervil Salad and Osetra Caviar

Alaskan Halibut with Red and Yellow Beets, Escargots, Parsnip Flan, and a Carrot Sauce

Scottish Woodpigeon Breast with Crêpes, Cauliflower Mushroom, Foie Gras,

Duck Proscuiutto and a Squab Glace

Chocolate Terrine with Cranberry, Rhum Crème Anglaise

Rover's

ROVER'S RESTAURANT
THIERRY RAUTUREAU
(THE CHEF IN THE HAT!!!™),
OWNER AND EXECUTIVE CHEF

2808 E MADISON
SEATTLE, WA 98112
206.325.7442
www.rovers-seattle.com

AWARD WINNING CHEF THIERRY RAUTUREAU, BELOVED LOCALLY AND respected internationally for his innovative cuisine, is celebrating his 17th year of ownership of the acclaimed Rover's Restaurant. Located in Seattle's Madison Valley, this intimate dining spot is nestled in a private courtyard and filled with art and warm sophistication—a trademark of the friendly "Chef in the Hat!!!"

James Beard Winner for "Best Chef in the Pacific Northwest," Thierry and Rover's have been recognized for several years running by the Zagat Survey, DiRoNa, AAA, and Mobil for outstanding food and service. Thierry personally was honored with the DiRoNa's Ella Brennan Distinguished Dining Ambassador Award which recognizes a representative of the restaurant industry who has exemplified and promoted the image of fine dining in America and abroad, and who has enhanced the image of fine dining nationally and internationally to the dining public and the dining press.

Included in the many honors the restaurant has received are *Seattle Magazine*'s "Best Chef in Seattle" and "All Time Favorite Restaurant," top honors from *WHERE* magazine, and a rare four-star rating from the *Seattle PI* and *Seattle Times*. Thierry hosts gourmands from all over the world at Rover's as they come to enjoy his innovative Northwest contemporary cuisine with a French accent.

Rover's Cookbook will be available in 2005

Scrambled Egg with Crème Fraîche and White Sturgeon Caviar

8 MEDIUM SIZE EGGS,
WHISK IN A BOWL
1 TBSP BUTTER
2 TSP SHALLOTS, FINELY CHOPPED
1 TSP THYME, CHOPPED
1 TSP CHIVES, SLICED
SEASON TO TASTE
3 TBSP CRÈME FRAÎCHE, WHIPPED
AND PUT IN A PASTRY BAG
WITH A MEDIUM-SIZE PLAIN TIP
2 OZ WHITE STURGEON CAVIAR
(OR ONE OF YOUR PREFERENCE)

SERVES 4

On top of a 1 3/8" round pastry cutter, place a triple-folded paper napkin. Sit an egg (larger end) on the napkin. Place a 1 1/4" round pastry cutter on top. With a heavy knife, tap slightly 2 or 3 times on the shell. Slowly remove the top part of the shell. Pour into a bowl and beat all eggs together. Rinse all the shells under cold water. Turn upside-down to dry.

In a pot, melt the butter. Add the shallots. Sweat for 2 minutes. Add the thyme. Mix and pour in the eggs. Slowly cook while mixing strongly until it becomes a creamy, runny texture. Remove from stove. Add the chives and pour back into the eggshell. Top with the crème fraîche by forming a circle toward the center of the egg. Top with white sturgeon caviar. Garnish with a chervil sprig.

124

Cured Troll King Salmon with a Parsley Root Chervil Salad and Osetra Caviar

8 OZ CURED SALMON (OR SMOKED
SALMON), SLICED THIN
2 OZ OSETRA CAVIAR
16 THIN SLICES OF BRIOCHE
(OR BREAD), TOASTED
1 CUP CHERVIL SPRIGS
2 CUPS PARSLEY ROOT, JULIENNED
(OR CELERY ROOT)
1 TBSP DIJON MUSTARD
2 TSP OLIVE OIL
SEASON TO TASTE

SERVES 4

In a bowl, mix the olive oil and the mustard thoroughly. Add the parsley root. Season to taste.

On a plate, lay out the salmon slices in a fan. Place the chervil at the tip of the fan and top with the parsley root salad. Put the toast on the side. Finish the presentation with dots of yellow bell pepper coulis. Place Osetra caviar at the end of each slice of smoked salmon. Serve.

Alaskan Halibut with
Red and Yellow Beets,
Escargots, Parsnip Flan,
and a Carrot Sauce

SERVES 4

❧ In a mixing bowl, pour the eggs and mix thoroughly. Add the parsnip purée while whisking. Pour the cream slowly while mixing. Season to taste.

Butter four 3 to 4 oz soufflé molds. Place molds in baking pan. Pour parsnip flan mixture into soufflé molds. Fill baking pan with hot water to reach halfway up molds. Cover tightly with foil. Bake in oven for about 25 minutes at 300°.

To check on the cooking of the flan, run a small knife blade through the center of the flan. If it comes out clean, it is ready. Let molds rest in the water bath for about 30 minutes. Remove flan from mold by running a knife blade around the inside of the mold.

In a hot skillet, add the olive oil and the butter. When golden in color, place the halibut in the pan. Slightly color and flip on the other side. Finish cooking in a 350° oven for about 3 to 4 minutes or until medium.

While cooking, bring the fish stock to a boil. Blend in the carrot purée and add the butter, whisking slowly. Keep warm.

In a hot sauté pan, melt the butter to a golden brown stage. Add the escargot and cook for about 1 minute while tossing in the pan. Add the shallots and garlic. Cook for another minute. Add the beets and cook for 2 minutes. Season to taste. Add the chives and set aside.

In the center of the plate, place the halibut. Place the beets and the escargot next to the halibut and the flan on the top part of the plate. Ladle the sauce around the fish and the vegetables. Serve warm.

2 OZ BUTTER
1 OZ MOROCCAN OLIVE OIL
16 OZ ALASKAN HALIBUT, CLEANED, SKINNED AND CUT INTO
4 EVEN PORTIONS
2 TBSP UNSALTED BUTTER
16 ESCARGOT (PETIT GRIS OR PETIT DE BOURGUOGNE)
1 TBSP SHALLOTS, CHOPPED
1/2 TSP GARLIC, CHOPPED
10 OZ BABY YELLOW BEETS, BOILED, SKINNED, AND QUARTERED

❧ PARSNIP FLAN
1 CUP PARSNIP PURÉE
1/2 CUP EGGS
1/2 CUP HEAVY CREAM
SALT AND PEPPER TO TASTE
8 OZ CURED SALMON (OR SMOKED SALMON), SLICED THIN
SEASON TO TASTE

1 CUP FISH STOCK
(REDUCED TO 1/4 CUP)
1/2 CUP CARROT PURÉE
1 TBSP UNSALTED BUTTER

125

Scottish Woodpigeon Breast with Crêpes, Cauliflower Mushroom, Foie Gras, Duck Prosciutto and a Squab Glace

2 TBSP UNSALTED BUTTER

4 WOODPIGEONS, BONED AND
CUT INTO 8 BREASTS AND 8 LEGS

2 1/2 TBSP UNSALTED BUTTER

1/4 CUP LOBSTER MUSHROOMS,
WASHED AND THINLY SLICED

1/4 CUP CAULIFLOWER MUSHROOMS,
WASHED AND THINLY SLICED

1 TBSP SHALLOTS, CHOPPED

1 TSP GARLIC, CHOPPED

1 TBSP CHIVES, CHOPPED

1/4 CUP DUCK PROSCIUTTO, JULIENNED
(OR PORK PROSCIUTTO)

8 OZ HUDSON VALLEY FOIE GRAS,
CUT INTO 1/4" THICK SLICES

3 CUPS SQUAB STOCK, REDUCED
DOWN TO 1/2 CUP

1 TBSP UNSALTED BUTTER

SERVES 4

In a hot sauté pan, melt the 2 tbsp of butter. Add the woodpigeon, skin side down. Sear until crisp, about 2 to 3 minutes. Flip over and cook for another 3 to 4 minutes. Set aside to rest.

In a hot sauté pan, melt the 2 1/2 tbsp of butter. When brown, add the lobster mushrooms. Cook for about 2 minutes. Add the cauliflower mushrooms. Cook for another 3 to 4 minutes, while tossing in the pan. Add the shallots and the garlic. Cook for 1 minute and set aside. Add the chives and prosciutto to the mushrooms and set aside.

In a very hot skillet (cast iron recommended), place your foie gras slices after salting heavily. Sear until brown. Flip the slices over, discard the fat, and finish cooking the foie gras for about 2 more minutes. Take the slices out of the pan and set aside where warm.

In the skillet, bring the squab stock to a boil. Whisk in the 1 tbsp of butter. Season to taste.

In the center of the plate, put all the mushrooms. Top with the sliced woodpigeon. Finish with sauce to cover the woodpigeon. Place the foie gras atop the sauce in the center of the plate.

Garnish with carrot coulis, parsley sprig, chives.

126

Chocolate Terrine with Cranberry, Rhum Crème Anglaise

Makes 1 half-moon shape mold, 15" long

SERVES 8-10

1/2 LB DARK BITTERSWEET CHOCOLATE,
CUT IN SMALL PIECES ABOUT 1/4" SQUARE.
SET ASIDE IN A BIG MIXING BOWL
1 1/4 CUP HEAVY WHIPPING CREAM
2 OZ LIGHT CORN SYRUP
2 OZ UNSALTED BUTTER,
DICED IN 1/2" CUBE
1/8 CUP GRAND MARNIER
(OR LIQUEUR OF YOUR CHOICE)

❧ In a pot, bring the cream and corn syrup to a boil. Slowly add the mixture to the chocolate. Blend thoroughly until incorporated. Add the butter a little at a time. When mixed thoroughly, add 1/8 cup liqueur slowly while whisking thoroughly. Pour into terrine mold and refrigerate for at least 3 to 4 hours.

Melt the other chocolate slowly, while mixing over a double boiler. Very slowly, add oil while mixing continuously. Add 1 oz liqueur very slowly while mixing. Once completely mixed, pour over the cold terrine. Refrigerate for at least 1 hour.

❧ GLAZE   127
10 OZ BITTERSWEET OR
WHITE CHOCOLATE,
CUT IN SMALL PIECES ABOUT
1/4" SQUARE.
SET ASIDE IN A BIG MIXING BOWL

To slice, use a blade warmed in hot water. Dry before using. Slice the terrine and place on a plate. Garnish with cranberries and Rhum Crème Anglaise.

2 OZ VEGETABLE OIL
1 OZ GRAND MARNIER

❧ RHUM CRÈME ANGLAISE
5 EGG YOLKS
1 1/4 CUP GRANULATED SUGAR
2 CUPS HEAVY CREAM
2 VANILLA BEANS
2 OZ DARK RUM

❧ In a pot, warm the cream. Scrape the vanilla beans. Stir the scrapes and the beans into the cream. In a bowl, mix egg yolks and sugar thoroughly. Pour the boiling cream into the egg and sugar mixture while blending fervently, only adding the cream a little bit at a time. When completely mixed, cook slowly over a double boiler until thickened and forms a "nappé" over a spatula. Make sure it does not boil or it will curdle. At the last minute, add the rum and mix. Strain through a fine sieve and cool over an ice bath.

❧ CANDIED CRANBERRIES
2 CUPS CRANBERRIES
2 CUPS SUGAR

❧ In a boiling pot of water, drop the cranberries. Cook for about 1 minute. Strain and cool, making sure the berries are dry. Roll into the sugar and let dry overnight on a draining rack. Serve as a garnish around the terrine.

Note: Some of the cranberries can be blended with a little water and used as a coulis for sauce around the terrine.

Wine Pairing

SCRAMBLED EGG WITH CRÈME FRAÎCHE AND WHITE STURGEON CAVIAR
DELILLE CELLARS 2002 CHALEUR ESTATE BLANC
COLUMBIA VALLEY WHITE
(Bordeaux Blend) Sauvignon Blanc/Semillon Blend

CURED TROLL KING SALMON WITH A PARSLEY ROOT
CHERVIL SALAD AND OSETRA CAVIAR
DELILLE CELLARS 2001 CHALEUR ESTATE
YAKIMA VALLEY RED
(Bordeaux Blend) Cabernet Sauvignon, Merlot,
Cabernet Franc and Petite Verdot

ALASKAN HALIBUT WITH RED AND YELLOW BEETS,
ESCARGOTS, PARSNIP FLAN, AND A CARROT SAUCE
DELILLE CELLARS 2001 D2
YAKIMA VALLEY RED
(Bordeaux Blend) Merlot, Cabernet Sauvignon,
Cabernet Franc and Petite Verdot

SCOTTISH WOODPIGEON BREAST WITH CRÊPES,
CAULIFLOWER MUSHROOM, FOIE GRAS,
DUCK PROSCIUTTO AND A SQUAB GLACE
DELILLE CELLARS 2001 HARRISON HILL
YAKIMA VALLEY SINGLE VINEYARD RED
(Bordeaux Blend) Cabernet Sauvignon, Merlot,
Cabernet Franc and Petite Verdot

CHOCOLATE TERRINE WITH
CRANBERRY, RHUM CRÈME ANGLAISE
DOYENNE 2002 SYRAH
YAKIMA VALLEY

128

FOUNDED IN 1992 BY CHARLES LILL, CHRIS UPCHURCH, GREG LILL, AND Jay Soloff, DeLille Cellars is an independently owned winery located in Woodinville, Washington. We built a traditional "chai" style winery on the Lill family farm. This beautiful ten-acre site sits above the Woodinville Valley floor and overlooks Chateau Ste. Michelle and Columbia Winery. As a family-owned winery, we have an uncompromising philosophy about the quality of each DeLille wine.

DeLille Cellars produces four Bordeaux-styled wines—Chaleur Estate Red, D2, Harrison Hill, and Chaleur Estate Blanc. We also feature a Northern Rhône-style Syrah we call 'Doyenne.' All wines from DeLille are made with the highest hand-crafted standards. Only grapes from the oldest and best vineyards in Washington State are acquired. Hand picked and hand sorted at crush, we use only the finest berry clusters. The traditional DeLille Cellars structure allows for winemaking methods used in the renowned chateaux of Bordeaux, including open-top fermenters and an underground barrel cellar. Our wines are never filtered and are aged in 100% new French Oak barrels every year.

DELILLE CELLARS

CHARLES LILL, CHRIS UPCHURCH, GREG LILL, JAY SOLOFF, OWNERS

14208 WOODINVILLE-REDMOND ROAD NE

REDMOND, WA 98052

425.489.0544

www.delillecellars.com

DeLille Cellars was named Winery of the Year 2000 by the *New York Times*. *The Wine Advocate* rated DeLille as one of the top four producers, bestowing the title "Lafite Rothschild of Washington State." *Decanter* placed our 1998 Chaleur Estate on their Pacific Northwest Top Ten List, giving it their highest rating of five stars and chose our 1999 Harrison Hill as a recommended Wine of the Month in May 2002. The Institute of the Masters of Wine in London, England also honored DeLille Cellars with the Certificate of Excellence Award, the only winery from the northwest to receive this honor. Six of the last seven years, the DeLille Cellars Chaleur Estate was awarded scores of 91-96 points, given a platinum medal, and was twice chosen one of the top 100 wines of the world by *Wine Enthusiast Magazine*. *Wine Spectator* rated the 1999 Chaleur Estate a score of 93 points and the 2000 Chaleur Estate a score of 91 points. In 1997, DeLille Cellars broke the record for the highest price paid for a bottle of Washington State wine at auction ($16,000).

Seafood Cioppino

Yellow and Red Bell Pepper Soup Side–by–Side with Basil Pistou

Macadamia Nut and Black Sesame Seed Crusted Salmon, Red Jasmine Rice,

Green Papaya Salad, Scallion Coulis

Chocolate Orange Brûleé Cake

Salty's

Salty's on Alki Beach
Gerry and Kathy Kingen,
Owners
Dan Thiessen,
Executive Chef

1936 Harbor Avenue SW
Seattle, WA 98126
206.937.1600
www.saltys.com

When asked about the best view of Seattle's shoreline, anyone who's been there will tell you it's from Salty's on Alki Beach. The incredible panorama from the Space Needle to Safeco Field, and from the Cascade Mountains to Mount Rainier, is the backdrop for feasting on delectable gifts from the sea. Sit at your table facing Elliott Bay as you watch the glittering sunset reflected on the Seattle skyline, shoot fresh oysters, break open crab legs, or enjoy a hearty prime steak prepared by Chef Dan Thiessen. Add a glass of L'Ecole N° 41 and you have an unparalleled dining experience at Salty's, a winner of the 2004 Award of Excellence by *Wine Spectator* magazine.

You can also enjoy an unbelievable Sunday brunch, rated the nation's best by MSN/Citysearch.com and Seattle's Best by the local media. There's a mind-numbing variety of fresh seafoods, crêpes and pasta dishes, carved beef, Eggs Benedict, homemade apple dumplings, pastries galore and even pink mimosas. After brunch, which is also available Saturdays, take the West Seattle water taxi across Elliott Bay for your day of exploring downtown Seattle or going to the ballpark.

Whether for sunset cocktails and dinner, a business lunch meant to impress, or that Sunday morning you've chosen to make special, Salty's offers you the place, the food, and the memories that will last until your next visit.

Seafood Cioppino

1/2 CUP CANOLA OIL

6 OZ ONION

4 OZ FENNEL

4 OZ EACH RED & GREEN PEPPER

1 OZ GARLIC

1 TSP RED CHILI FLAKES

1 SPRIG THYME

1/2 TBSP GROUND FENNEL SEEDS

1 OZ TOMATO PASTE

12 OZ ROMA TOMATOES

3/4 CUP RED WINE

3 CUPS FISH STOCK OR WATER

1/2 LB SALMON

1/2 LB PRAWNS

1 LB MUSSELS

1 LB CLAMS

1/2 LB SCALLOPS

1 PRECOOKED DUNGENESS CRAB

1 CUP DRY SHERRY

6 OZ BUTTER

SERVES 6

In a heavy bottomed pot, warm 1/4 cup canola oil over medium heat. Add onion, fennel, red and green peppers, and garlic. Cook until the vegetables are slightly soft. Add red chili flakes, thyme, and fennel seeds. Cook for 1 more minute.

Add tomato paste and diced Roma tomatoes. Deglaze the pan with wine. Cook for 5 minutes. Add fish stock and bring to a boil. Reduce heat and simmer for 3 minutes. You have the base for the Cioppino stew. Set aside.

In a large soup pot, heat the remaining 1/4 cup canola oil over medium heat. Add the diced salmon, prawns, mussels, clams, scallops, and crab.

Note: Chef Thiessen says you don't have to use only the seafood listed here. You can substitute with almost any type of seafood in this stew.

Pour in the base from the other pot and cover. Cook for at least 4 minutes until all of the clams and mussels steam open. Deglaze the pan with sherry and finish with butter. Serve with a thick hearty Focaccia bread.

Yellow and Red Bell Pepper Soup Side-by-Side with Basil Pistou

4 CUPS RED BELL PEPPER, SEEDED AND DICED

4 CUPS YELLOW BELL PEPPER, SEEDED AND DICED

1/4 CUP TOMATO PASTE

1/8 TSP SAFFRON

1/2 CUP ONION, PEELED AND DICED

1/4 CUP CARROT, PEELED AND DICED

1/4 CUP CELERY, DICED

2 TBSP SHALLOT, PEELED AND DICED

SERVES 6-8

On medium heat in two medium saucepans, add oil equally. Heat. Add onion, carrot, celery, and shallot equally and sweat until translucent. In one of the pans, add the tomato paste and cook out. Add the red bell peppers to the pan with the tomato paste. Add the yellow peppers to the other pan and sauté lightly. Add equal amounts of chicken stock, thyme, pepper, and bay leaf to each pan. Add the saffron to the pan with the yellow peppers and simmer both pans until peppers are soft. With an immersion blender, blend each soup until completely soft. Strain into separate containers. Stir in equal amounts of crème fraîche and butter. Season with salt and pepper. Adjust acidity with a pinch of sugar, if necessary. Keep warm.

❖ Combine all ingredients in a blender and blend until smooth. Keep chilled.

1/4 CUP OLIVE OIL
1 TSP DRY THYME
1 TSP PEPPERCORNS, CRACKED
6 BAY LEAVES
2 QTS WHITE CHICKEN STOCK
1/2 GALLON HEAVY CREAM,
REDUCED BY TWO-THIRDS
4 OZ BUTTER
6 OZ CRÈME FRAÎCHE
SUGAR, IF NEEDED
SALT AND PEPPER

❖ BASIL TOMATO PISTOU
1 CUP FRESH BASIL LEAVES
1/4 CUP PARMESAN CHEESE
3/4 CUP EXTRA VIRGIN OLIVE OIL
1 TBSP GARLIC, CHOPPED
1/2 CUP TOMATOES, CHOPPED,
PEELED AND SEEDED
SALT AND PEPPER

133

Macadamia Nut and Black Sesame Seed Crusted Salmon, Red Jasmine Rice, Green Papaya Salad, Scallion Coulis

SERVES 4

Combine nuts, sesame seeds, and panko. Mix well. Coat each piece of seasoned salmon with a liberal amount of nut mixture. Roast in a 350° oven until done, approximately 10 minutes.

4 8 OZ SALMON FILETS, SKIN REMOVED
1/2 CUP UNSALTED MACADAMIA NUTS,
ROUGHLY CHOPPED
2 TBSP BLACK SESAME SEEDS
1/2 CUP PANKO
SALT AND PEPPER

❖ Combine salt, coconut milk, and water together in a medium saucepan on high heat. Bring to a boil. When boiling, add rice and stir well. Return to a boil. Reduce heat to low, cover, and steam for 40 minutes.

❖ RED JASMINE RICE
2 CUPS RED RICE
1 1/2 CUPS COCONUT MILK
1 1/2 CUPS WATER
1 TBSP SALT

❖ GREEN PAPAYA SALAD

2 CUPS GREEN PAPAYA, SHREDDED

1/4 CUP SCALLION, SLICED

1/4 CUP CILANTRO, ROUGHLY CHOPPED

1 TBSP GINGER, PEELED AND MINCED

3 TBSP FRESH LIME JUICE

1/2 CUP OLIVE OIL

SALT AND PEPPER

❖ SCALLION COULIS

1 CUP SCALLION, CHOPPED

1 TBSP GINGER, PEELED AND CHOPPED

1 TBSP JALAPEÑO, SEEDED AND CHOPPED

1/4 CUP CILANTRO, CHOPPED

2 TBSP SUGAR

1/2 TBSP GARLIC, CHOPPED

3 TBSP RICE WINE VINEGAR

3 TBSP FRESH LIME JUICE

2 TBSP SESAME OIL

1/2 CUP VEGETABLE OIL

SALT AND PEPPER

❖ Combine all ingredients and season to taste.

❖ Combine all ingredients in a blender except for the sesame and vegetable oil. Blend until smooth. Slowly add sesame and vegetable oil to form an emulsion

Place 1 cup of rice on a warm plate to hold the fish. Add some papaya salad atop the fish and spoon 3 tbsp of coulis around the plate. Garnish with cilantro leaves and black sesame seeds.

134

Chocolate Orange Brûleé Cake

❖ ORANGE CRÈME BRÛLEÉ LAYER

5 OZ HEAVY CREAM

1/2 OZ ORANGE JUICE

1/2 OZ COINTREAU

PINCH ORANGE ZEST

2 EGG YOLKS

2 OZ (1/4 CUP) SUGAR

1/4 TSP GELATIN (GRANULAR)

❖ CHOCOLATE MOUSSE

1 QT HEAVY CREAM

3 WHOLE EGGS

1/2 CUP SUGAR

1 LB SEMI-SWEET CHOCOLATE

SERVES 8

❖ Bloom gelatin in cold water, set aside. Combine cream, orange juice, Cointreau, and zest in a small heavy bottom saucepan. Bring to a boil. Remove from heat.

Combine egg yolks and sugar. Add 1/3 of the hot liquid to egg yolks and sugar, whisking as you add. Return all to the hot liquid and heat, stirring constantly until it coats the back of a spoon. Add gelatin. Stir to dissolve. Pour into 8" cake pan lined with plastic wrap. Freeze. Best prepared a day ahead.

❖ Melt chocolate over hot water or in microwave. Keep warm, not hot. Whip heavy cream to medium stiff peaks. Cook sugar with 1/4 cup water to softball stage. Whisk into whole eggs. Keep whisking until just warm, not hot. Wisk in melted chocolate. Fold into whipped cream. Refrigerate until needed.

✤ Melt butter. Keep liquid warm, not hot. Combine sugar and flour. Add butter and combine to smooth. Do not overmix. Add eggs, one at a time, making sure mixture is smooth. Stir baking soda into buttermilk. Add to cake batter. Bake in three 8" pans at 325° for 20 to 25 minutes. Cool cakes on cake rack 5 minutes. Invert out of pans and cool completely. Freeze. (This makes it easier to cut later.)

This recipe makes more than you need so you will have some extra cake for another project.

✤ Bring to a boil, turn off. Reserve 1 1/2 cups for glaze and the rest for Cointreau syrup.

✤ Bring half and half and corn syrup to a boil. Chop chocolate bark and bittersweet chocolate into small (dime size) pieces. Put in large stainless steel bowl. Mix cocoa powder and 1 1/2 cups hot simple syrup. Whisk until smooth with no lumps. Pour hot half and half mixture over chopped chocolate. Stir with whisk until smooth and shiny and all chocolate is melted. Stir in cocoa powder mixture. Cool to about 100°.

✤ CHOCOLATE CAKE
2 CUPS FLOUR
2 CUPS SUGAR
2 EGGS
1 TSP BAKING SODA
1 CUP BUTTERMILK
1/2 LB (2 STICKS) BUTTER, MELTED

✤ SIMPLE SYRUP
1 CUP WATER
1 1/3 CUP SUGAR
1/2 CUP CORN SYRUP

✤ GLAZE
1 2/3 CUP HALF AND HALF
1/3 CUP CORN SYRUP
1 1/2 CUP SIMPLE SYRUP
1/2 LB CHOCOLATE BARK
(COATING CHOCOLATE)
1 LB BITTERSWEET CHOCOLATE
1/4 CUP DARK COCOA POWDER

TO ASSEMBLE CAKE

Remove two layers of cake from freezer. Cut off rounded tops so you have even layers. Discard top and set layers aside. Line 8" cake ring with plastic cake strip. Place one layer of cake on bottom, centered in cake ring. Brush with Cointreau syrup. Top with 1 1/2 cup mousse. Smooth out with small metal offset spatula.

Add second layer of cake, brush with Cointreau syrup. Top cake with brûleé layer. Fill remaining spaces with mousse. Level off the mousse with a long metal spatula. Freeze solid.

GLAZE

Glaze frozen cake over a screen rack on a sheet pan. Transfer immediately to cake plate or stand. Garnish with candied orange peel and orange macaroon cookies. Serve.

Wine Pairing

CIOPPINO
2002 SEVEN HILLS VINEYARD ESTATE SEMILLON

YELLOW AND RED BELL PEPPER SOUP
SIDE-BY-SIDE WITH BASIL PISTOU
2002 COLUMBIA VALLEY CHARDONNAY

MACADAMIA NUT AND BLACK SESAME SEED CRUSTED SALMON,
RED JASMINE RICE, GREEN PAPAYA SALAD, SCALLION COULIS
2002 SEVEN HILLS VINEYARD ESTATE MERLOT

CHOCOLATE ORANGE BRÛLÉE CAKE
2002 SEVEN HILLS VINEYARD LATE HARVEST SEMILLON

136

L'ECOLE Nº 41 HAS BEEN PRODUCING PREMIUM, HANDCRAFTED VARIETAL wines in the Walla Walla Valley since 1983 in the historic Frenchtown School. A family owned business, L'Ecole Nº 41 was founded by Jean and Baker Ferguson. Today the winery is owned and operated by their daughter and son-in-law, Megan and Martin Clubb.

Built in 1915, the schoolhouse is located in historic Frenchtown, thirteen miles west of Walla Walla. It derived its name from the many French-Canadians who settled the valley during the early 1800s. Legend has it, these settlers were raising grapes and producing wine. By the 1860s, nurseries, vineyards, and winemaking had become a part of the region's growing economy. The name—L'Ecole Nº 41—French for "the school" located in district 41, was chosen to salute the viticulture efforts of these early pioneers.

We are proud of our rich history and longevity making wines in the Walla Walla Valley; our dedication to making premium varietal wines from some of Washington's best vineyards; our commitment to superior vineyard management and environmentally sustainable vineyard practices; and our desire to provide our valuable customers with a unique, quality experience year after year.

L'Ecole Nº 41 was selected by *Wine Press Northwest* as the 2004 Pacific Northwest Winery of the Year. Other accolades include having a wine named to *Wine Spectator*'s Top 100 Wines of the Year each of the past three years and being named Regional Winery of the Year for the past two years by *Wine & Spirits*.

L'ECOLE Nº 41

MEGAN AND MARTIN CLUBB, OWNERS

41 LOWDEN SCHOOL ROAD
LOWDEN, WA 99360
509.525.0940
www.lecole.com

Roasted Andouille Clams with Spicy Tomato Broth

Sweet Corn and Dungeness Crab Chowder

Flash Fried Catfish with Jalapeno–Lime Menuiere

Blackberry Brioche Bread Pudding

Sazerac

SAZERAC
JASON McCLURE,
EXECUTIVE CHEF

1101 FOURTH AVENUE

SEATTLE, WA 98101

206.624.7755

www.sazerac-seattle.com

SAZERAC GETS ITS NAME FROM A TRADITIONAL NEW ORLEANS MIX OF RYE, bitters, simple syrup, and anise-flavored liqueur swirled together for a drink reminiscent of a slightly decadent lifestyle. The restaurant is that same snazzy blend of jazz and blues, setting the mood with handcrafted steel-framed chandeliers high overhead, illuminating the elevated kitchen and the dining room with its mahogany booths and velvet curtains.

Savory breads and desserts are hearth-baked. The chef's staff generally calls McClure "Pillsbury" because of his tasty, homemade, artisan breads. His cast iron cornbread skillets produce some of the best cornbread in town.

McClure's menu tickles the fancy as well as the palette with offerings such as porter-house steak with soft and sexy grits, pickled cabbage, and red-eye gravy. Many of the meats are smoked and cured in-house. Also served are good ol' crab cakes with spicy harissa mayonnaise, shaved fennel salad, and warm ooey-gooey chocolate cake with pouring cream. As McClure says, "We're so fortunate here in the Northwest; the quality of product in this area is incredible. My focus is on getting the best and most beautiful ingredients I can." And at Sazerac, it shows.

Roasted Andouille Clams with Spicy Tomato Broth

❖ TOMATOES

6 ROMA TOMATOES,
SLICED 1/2" THICK

❖ 2 LBS FRESH LIVE MANILA
OR OTHER SMALL TO MEDIUM
SIZED CLAM, WASHED
1/2 LB ANDOUILLE SAUSAGE,
SLICED INTO 1/4" ROUNDS
8 CLOVES GARLIC, SLICED
2 SHALLOTS, SLICED
1 LARGE YELLOW ONION, SLICED,
CARAMELIZED AND SET ASIDE
4-6 CUPS LIGHT CHICKEN STOCK
OR FUMET
2 CUP WHITE WINE
1 BUNCH PARSLEY,
ROUGH CHOPPED
1 BUNCH BASIL,
LEAVES PICKED WHOLE
4 TBSP BUTTER, PLUS ADDITIONAL
FOR SAUTÉ
TABASCO AND LEMON JUICE
(TO ADJUST HEAT AND ACIDITY)

SERVES 4

❖ Drizzle tomatoes with olive oil, salt and pepper, garlic and thyme. Oven roast at 250° until slightly softened and sweet.

❖ Heat a large sauté pan or straight sided pot (large enough to accommodate the clams) over high heat and add butter. Once the butter has melted, add the Andouille sausage and cook until partially rendered. Add garlic and shallot, cooking briefly, until slightly caramelized. Add caramelized onions, clams, and tomatoes, crushing them between your fingers. Add salt, pepper, and white wine.

Cover the clams and allow to steam until almost all of the white wine has evaporated. Add chicken stock. Cover again until all of the clams have opened, approximately 1 to 2 minutes. Remove the lid one more time and allow the stock to reduce slightly to create a sauce.

Adjust salt and pepper, tabasco, and lemon juice to taste. Toss in the chopped parsley. Divide evenly in four bowls. Tear fresh basil over the top of each. Serve immediately with plenty of crusty bread for dipping.

140

Sweet Corn and Dungeness Crab Chowder

SERVES 12-16

Render the bacon. Pour off all fat except for 2 tbsp. Add butter, onions, peppers, thyme, cumin and tumeric. Sweat until tender, 5 to 10 minutes. Add the potatoes, corn, and stock. Bring to a boil. Boil hard for 10 minutes. Reduce heat and continue to cook until the potatoes are soft and just starting to break down. Whisk together cornstarch and 1 cup of water. Stir into soup mixture. Return to boil to activate the cornstarch. Reduce heat to simmer and add cream. Season to taste.

1 GALLON SHUCKED CORN
2 LBS BACON, DICED
2 TBSP BUTTER
4 RED ONIONS, DICED
4 YELLOW ONIONS, DICED
6 RED BELL PEPPERS, DICED
4 TSP GROUND CUMIN
1 TSP TUMERIC
2 TBSP THYME, CHOPPED
8 LBS YUKON POTATOES, DICED LARGE
1 GALLON SHELLFISH AND CORN STOCK
4 TBSP CORNSTARCH
1 CUP WATER
8 CUPS CREAM

Flash Fried Catfish with Jalapeño-Lime Menuiere

SERVES 4

4 6-7 OZ FILETS OF CATFISH
2 CUPS BUTTERMILK

✤ Place the catfish in a bowl and cover with buttermilk. Transfer catfish to a dish of cornmeal dredge. Coat fish completely. Fry catfish in peanut oil at 350° until crisp and golden brown, about 3 minutes. Place on a platter with paper towels to drain while the sauce is made.

✤ CORNMEAL DREDGE
1 CUP FLOUR
1 CUP SEMOLINA
SALT AND PEPPER TO TASTE

✤ Place 1 tbsp of butter in a sauté pan over high heat. As the butter starts to melt, it will foam. As the foam subsides, the butter will take on a light brown color and a wonderful hazelnut aroma. Add garlic, shallots, and jalapeño. Sauté in the butter until garlic and shallots are nicely toasted and golden brown. Add a healthy squirt of lime juice, Worcestershire, and tabasco. Season with salt and pepper. Add remaining 2 tbsp of butter and stir constantly until the butter is melted. Transfer catfish to serving platter and pour sauce over the top. Serve immediately.

✤ JALAPEÑO-LIME MENUIERE
3 TBSP BUTTER
1 CLOVE GARLIC, MINCED
1/2 SHALLOT, MINCED
1/4 JALAPEÑO, MINCED
LIME JUICE
WORCESTERSHIRE
TABASCO
SALT AND PEPPER TO TASTE

141

142

Blackberry Brioche Bread Pudding

SERVES 6-8

Cube brioche and set aside.

✤ Mix all ingredients for the custard and set aside.

✤ Mix all ingredients for the fruit mixture and set aside.

Spread half of the brioche in an ovenproof dish. Spoon the fruit mixture over the brioche. Add the rest of the brioche, if needed, over the fruit mixture, creating a layered effect. Pour the custard over the whole thing, a little at a time, until the custard is gone or the dish can hold no more.

Allow to soak in the refrigerator for several hours or overnight.

Bake in a water bath, covered, 300° for approximately 1 hour or until a knife inserted into the middle comes out clean. Serve with a dollop of Chantilly or your favorite ice cream.

2 LOAVES BRIOCHE (YOUR FAVORITE), CUT IN 1" CUBES

✤ CUSTARD
5 EGG YOLKS
2 WHOLE EGGS
2 CUPS SUGAR
4 CUPS CREAM
1 VANILLA BEAN
PINCH OF SALT

✤ FRUIT MIXTURE
1 PINT BLACKBERRIES, PURÉED WITH 1/2 CUP HONEY
1/3 CUP SUGAR
1 VANILLA BEAN
PINCH OF BLACK PEPPER
2 PINTS BLACKBERRIES, ROUGHLY CHOPPED

143

Wine Pairing

ROASTED ANDOUILLE CLAMS WITH SPICY TOMATO BROTH
2002 PINOT NOIR HOODVIEW VINEYARD
WILLAMETTE VALLEY

SWEET CORN AND DUNGENESS CRAB CHOWDER
2003 VIOGNIER CLIFTON VINEYARD
COLUMBIA VALLEY

FLASH FRIED CATFISH WITH JALAPEÑO–LIME MENUIERE
2002 SYRAH SUNDANCE VINEYARD
COLUMBIA VALLEY

BLACKBERRY BRIOCHE BREAD PUDDING
2002 SYRAH MINICK VINEYARD
YAKIMA VALLEY

144

AFTER FIFTEEN YEARS AS A SUCCESSFUL CHEF AND RESTAURATEUR, ROBERT Goodfriend felt it was time for a change. He began his winemaking apprenticeship in California's central coast wine region. In 1995, Robert moved to Oregon to work with Pinot Noir. A fortuitous trip to a Seattle wine event led Robert to meet his future bride. One year later, Robert and Elizabeth were married. In 1998, they built and bonded Harlequin Wine Cellars. At Harlequin, Robert and Elizabeth personally oversee all aspects of the 1800 case production

With great respect for time-honored, traditional winemaking and up-to-date technology, Harlequin strives to create wines of individuality and substance, working with outstanding vineyards and growers in Washington and Oregon. Individual rows in the best vineyards are designated to Harlequin.

The winemaking at Harlequin is hands-on and intensive. All lots are vinified separately. Reds are fermented in small one ton fermentors and punched down by hand. Whites are pressed whole-cluster and are barrel-fermented. Only the best barrels from the best suppliers are used. Wines are topped up every six weeks and are left alone to evolve and gain complexity.

"At Harlequin we care most about producing wines of ultrapremium quality. We strive to be proud of every bottle of wine we produce." —Robert Goodfriend

HARLEQUIN

WINE CELLARS

ROBERT GOODFRIEND AND
ELIZABETH COOK,
OWNERS

1211 SAND PIT ROAD

TOUCHET, WA 99360

509.394.2112

www.harlequinwine.com

Steamed Clams with Pesto

Blue Cheese, Shrimp and Pear Salad

Reggiano Parmigiano Crusted Halibut

Banana Spring Roll Sundae

Seastar

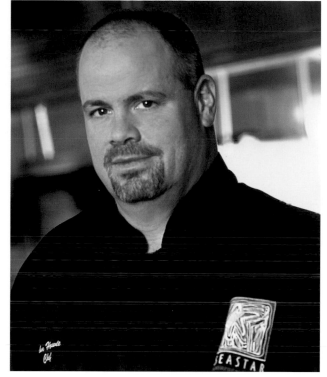

SEASTAR RESTAURANT
AND RAW BAR
JOHN HOWIE,
OWNER AND EXECUTIVE CHEF

205 108TH AVENUE NE
BELLEVUE, WA 98004
425.456.0010
www.seastarrestaurant.com

CHEF JOHN HOWIE'S SEASTAR RESTAURANT AND RAW BAR OPENED IN 2002 to incredible accolades, a four star review and was voted the "Best New Restaurant in Western Washington" by the viewers of KING 5 Evening Magazine in 2003.

Chef Howie uses only the finest ingredients the Pacific Northwest has to offer, creating an amazing array of freshly prepared dishes. Enjoy the luxurious Seastar dining room where the aroma of cedar plank-roasted salmon fills the air, or listen to the sizzle of the 1800° broiler where Kobe Beef and Kurobuta Pork are cooked to perfection.

Stop in the Seastar Raw Bar where you can watch the chef prepare fresh shucked oysters, sushi, sashimi, ceviche, pokes, tartares, and incredible seafood towers with crab, shrimp, and scallops all while you sip on one of Seastar's famous specialty cocktails.

Under the direction of Star Sommelier Erik Liedholm, Seastar has received great recognition for their wine program. The July 2003 issue of *FOOD & WINE Magazine* named Seastar's wine list "Best New Wine List in America" and, in August 2003, they received the *Wine Spectator* Award of Excellence.

Seastar shines bright like a star with excellent service and uncompromised quality in a timeless setting.

Steamed Clams with Pesto

1 LB CLAMS IN SHELL,
SMALL MANILA OR BUTTER CLAMS

1/2 FL OZ OLIVE OIL

3/4 TSP GARLIC, MINCED

1/4 TSP CRUSHED RED CHILIS

1 FL OZ CLAM JUICE

1 FL OZ WHITE WINE

1/4 CUP SWEET BASIL PESTO
(RECIPE FOLLOWS)

1 TBSP PINE NUTS, TOASTED

2 SLICES REGGIANO PARMIGIANO,
SHAVED

SERVES 4

Place the olive oil, chilis, and garlic over medium heat in a sauté pan. Sauté 1 to 2 minutes until garlic begins to turn golden.

Deglaze pan with clam juice and white wine. When liquid begins to boil, add clams. Reduce heat to low and cover with a basting cover.

Cook 2 to 3 minutes until clams just begin to open. Add the pesto.

Let cook lightly until sauce just begins to thicken. Place in heated bowl. Garnish with pine nuts and shaved Parmagiano. Serve.

✤ BASIL PESTO

2 TBSP FRESH BASIL,
COARSELY CHOPPED

1 TBSP FRESH PARSLEY,
COARSELY CHOPPED

1/2 TSP GARLIC, MINCED

1 1/2 TSP PINE NUTS, TOASTED

1/16 TSP KOSHER SALT

1 1/2 TSP REGGIANO PARMIGIANO
CHEESE, GRATED

1 1/2 TSP WHOLE SALTED BUTTER

1 TBSP OLIVE OIL

✤ Combine all ingredients, except butter and oil, in a food processor and pulse. Process until ingredients are finely chopped but not pureéd to mush. Add the butter and oil and process to a thick paste.

Blue Cheese, Shrimp and Pear Salad

SERVES 4

❖ Cut the endive and radicchio in half. Baste with olive oil. Place on a preheated grill pan and grill on both sides. Achieve some grill marks. Don't let it get soft. Remove from the grill and cool on a sheet tray in a refrigerator. Cut the radicchio and the endive. Toss together and refrigerate until ready to serve.

❖ Place all the wet ingredients except cheese into a large mixing bowl with the paddle attachment. Mix on low speed for 1 to 2 minutes. Add all the remaining ingredients except cheese. Mix 1 minute. Add the cheese and blend for 1 to 2 minutes. Transfer, label, and hold refrigerated for 24 hours to allow flavors to blend.

WHEN READY

Toss the romaine, endive, and grilled mix with the dressing until completely coated. Place on the plate and top with hazelnuts, shrimp, tomatoes, and blue cheese crumbles. Julienne slice the pears 1/8" x 1/8" x 1-1 1/2" and place on top of the salad. Serve.

8 OZ ROMAINE, CUT 3/4" JULIENNE, HEARTS ONLY
4 OZ CURLY ENDIVE, CUT 1/2" JULIENNE
4 OZ GRILLED RADICCHIO-BELGIAN ENDIVE MIX (RECIPE FOLLOWS)
8 FL OZ BLUE CHEESE DRESSING (RECIPE FOLLOWS)
2 OZ TOASTED HAZELNUTS
4 OZ BAY SHRIMP
4 OZ SWEET "100" TOMATOES
2 OZ BLUE CHEESE CRUMBLES
8 OZ FRESH CRISP PEAR, JULIENNE SLICED 1/8" X 1/8" X 1-2"

❖ GRILLED RADICCHIO-ENDIVE MIX
YIELDS 4 OZ
1 TBSP OLIVE OIL, FOR BASTING THE VEGETABLE BEFORE GRILLING
1/2 HEAD RADICCHIO, CUT IN HALF, GRILLED, SLICED 1/4" X 1-2" LONG
1 HEAD BELGIAN ENDIVE, CUT IN HALF, GRILLED, THEN CUT CROSSWISE IN 1/4" SLICES,

❖ BLUE CHEESE DRESSING
YIELDS 2 CUPS
1/2 TSP FRESH GARLIC, MINCED VERY FINE
1/4 TSP DRY MUSTARD, COLEMAN'S BRAND
1/4 BLACK PEPPER, COARSE GROUND
1/2 TSP ONION, GRANULATED
PINCH OF GROUND WHITE PEPPER
1 TBSP RED WINE VINEGAR
1/4 TSP WORCESTERSHIRE SAUCE
1/3 CUP SOUR CREAM
1 CUP MAYONNAISE
1/4 CUP BUTTERMILK
4 OZ BLUE CHEESE, 1/4" CHUNKS, MAYTAG BRAND

149

Reggiano Parmigiano Crusted Halibut

8 HALIBUT FILETS, CUT INTO THIN
MEDALLIONS 2 1/2- 3 OZ EACH

1/2 TSP SALT

1/2 TSP PEPPER

1 EGG

1/3 CUP MILK

2 1/2 OZ REGGIANO PARMIGIANO
CHEESE, GRATED

1 1/2 OZ ASIAGO CHEESE, GRATED

1 1/2 OZ BREAD CRUMBS, FINE

1/4 CUP CLARIFIED BUTTER

4 FL OZ CREAMY BUTTER SAUCE*

1 TBSP LEMON-CHIVE OIL*

*(RECIPE FOLLOWS)

4 CHERVIL SPRIGS

❖ CREAMY BUTTER SAUCE
YIELDS 1/2 CUP

1 FL. OZ WHIPPING CREAM

2 OZ WHOLE SALTED BUTTER

2 OZ WHOLE UNSALTED BUTTER

❖ LEMON-CHIVE OIL
YIELD 1/4 CUP

1/4 CUP OLIVE OIL, E.V.

2 TBSP FRESH CHIVES, CUT 2'' SECTIONS,
SHOCKED IN BOILING WATER FOR
5 SECONDS, THEN IMMEDIATELY COOLED

1 TSP FRESH LEMON ZEST

1 1/2 TSP FRESH LEMON JUICE

150

SERVES 4

Prepare before needed.

Mix the egg and milk together until blended, set aside. In a food processor, blend the cheeses and bread crumbs until powdered. Set aside. Season the filets evenly with salt and pepper. Dip the filets into the egg wash and press them into the cheese mixture. Hold refrigerated until needed.

❖ Place cream in a sauce pot and bring to a slow boil, let it reduce by 25%. Slowly add the butter to the cream until it is completely dissolved (if the sauce is too thick at this point, you may slowly stir in some warm water to thin sauce to proper consistency). Transfer and hold warm until needed.

❖ Combine all ingredients together in a food processor and process until completely pureéd. Strain through a fine mesh strainer. Transfer and hold in a squeeze bottle until needed.

WHEN READY

Place clarified butter on a flat top grill or non-stick sauté pan. Cook until the topping is golden brown. Turn and cook until temperature of 120° is achieved. Remove from the searing grill or sauté pan and place filets slightly overlapping on the plate. Pour the butter sauce over the top of the fish. Place dots of the lemon-chive oil around the plate. Garnish with the chervil sprig. Serve with vegetables and potatoes, if desired.

Banana Spring Roll Sundae

SERVES 4

❖ Lay the sheets of spring roll wrappers out, corner at the top. Roll the banana slices in sugar until completely coated on the exterior. Shake off excess sugar and place the banana at the bottom corner. Press lightly and shape to straighten.

Place 2 tsp of shredded coconut on each banana, letting it fall on both sides of the banana in the wrapper. Take the bottom corner of the wrapper and fold over the top of the banana. Tuck under the banana and tighten.

Baste the two sides of the wrap as well as on top of the banana with the egg whites. Take the sides and stick them up on top of the banana. Baste the remaining area of the wrapper and roll up tightly. Transfer, label, and hold refrigerated until needed.

❖ Mix all ingredients together and hold at room temperature until needed.

❖ Combine the sugar, salt, and water and cook until the sugar is caramelized to a rich golden brown. Slowly add the cream, whisking constantly. Cook for 2 to 3 minutes. Hold warm until needed.

❖ Mix diced fruit and sugar together in a bowl and toss lightly. Hold refrigerated until needed.

WHEN READY

Place the spring roll in the fryer and cook for 2 to 3 minutes until golden brown. Remove from fryer and roll in the cinnamon/allspice sugar until well coated. Shake off excess. Slice in half diagonally, using a serrated knife.

Place one scoop of ice cream in a martini glass. Place the sliced banana spring roll on the back side of the martini glass. Add a second scoop of ice cream. Drizzle the caramel sauce over the ice cream and the bottom of the spring roll. Top with the pineapple relish. Garnish with a kaffir lime leaf or a pineapple leaf spear. Serve in a martini glass.

---

4 BANANA-COCONUT SPRING ROLLS
(RECIPE FOLLOWS)

16 FL OZ (8 SCOOPS)
VANILLA ICE CREAM

3 TBSP CINNAMON-ALLSPICE SUGAR
(RECIPE FOLLOWS)

6 FL OZ CARAMEL SAUCE
(RECIPE FOLLOWS)

1/2 CUP PINEAPPLE RELISH
(RECIPE FOLLOWS)

4 KAFFIR LIME LEAF OR
PINEAPPLE LEAF

❖ BANANA-COCONUT
SPRING ROLLS

4 BANANAS CUT INTO 4" PORTIONS,
SKINNED

2 TBSP + 2 TSP UNSWEETENED
COCONUT, CHOPPED OR SHREDDED

2 TBSP GRANULATED SUGAR

4 SPRING OR EGG ROLL WRAPPERS

2 EGG WHITES, LIGHTLY WHIPPED

❖ CINNAMON-ALLSPICE
SUGAR

YIELDS 4 TBSP

1/4 CUP GRANULTED SUGAR

1/2 TSP GROUND ALLSPICE

1/2 TSP GROUND CINNAMON

❖ CARAMEL SAUCE

YIELDS 1 CUP

3/4 CUP GRANULATED SUGAR

2 TBSP WATER

1/4 TSP KOSHER SALT

6 TBSP HEAVY CREAM

❖ SWEET PINEAPPLE RELISH

YIELDS 1/2 CUP

1/2 CUP FRESH GOLD PINEAPPLE
SKINNED, CORED AND DICED 1/4"

1 TBSP GRANULATED SUGAR

151

STEAMED CLAMS WITH PESTO
2002 INLAND DESERT ROSE

BLUE CHEESE, SHRIMP AND PEAR SALAD
2001 KLIPSUN VINEYARD SAUVIGNON BLANC

REGGIANO PARMIGIANO CRUSTED HALIBUT
2000 YAKIMA VALLEY RED WINE

BANANA SPRING ROLL SUNDAE
2001 ELERDING VINEYARD LATE HARVEST VIOGNIER

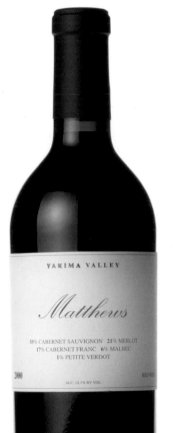

YAKIMA VALLEY

Matthews

**53% CABERNET SAUVIGNON   28% MERLOT
19% CABERNET FRANC**

1998

ALC. 13.4% BY VOL.

RED WINE

MATTHEWS

CELLARS

MATTHEW LOSO,
WINEMAKER

16116 140TH PLACE NE

WOODINVILLE, WA 98072

425.487.9810

www.matthewscellars.com

MATTHEWS CELLARS IS LOCATED ON AN EIGHT-ACRE ESTATE IN THE TOWN of Woodinville, Washington. Winemaker and owner, Matthew Loso, concentrates his efforts on production of a red blend using only the traditional Bordeaux varietals. These wines are from grapes grown in select Columbia Valley vineyards.

Matthew became interested in winemaking at the age of eighteen. After interning at several Washington State wineries, he set out to create his first vintage of Matthews Cellars in 1993. Matthews Cellars has grown quickly and is approaching its twelfth vintage of the Yakima Valley Red Wine. Last year, with its 2003 release, Matthews Cellars was awarded 91 points by *Wine Spectator* magazine. Despite his grand success and growth, Matthew continues to oversee and personally manage each and every part of production. This personal attention ensures only the highest level of quality winemaking every step of the way. Connoisseurs describe his wine as possessing elegance and finesse, not often seen in New World wines.

"Inky dark ruby in the glass, layers and layers of fruit and oak in the nose, and ripe, rich flavors of exotic spices, blueberry, plush black cherry, cassis and cedar."

Gnocchi di Semolino

Zuppa di Castagne (Chestnut Soup)

Serafina Calamari

Profiteroles with Bittersweet Chocolate Sauce

Serafina

SERAFINA
SUSAN KAUFMAN,
OWNER
JOHN NEUMARK,
EXECUTIVE CHEF

2043 EASTLAKE AVENUE E
SEATTLE, WA 98102
206.323.0807
www.serafinaseattle.com

SERAFINA OPENED ITS DOORS IN 1991 AS AN INTIMATE NEIGHBORHOOD restaurant located along Eastlake between the University of Washington and downtown Seattle. Its ochre walls, reminiscent of the Tuscan landscape, along with its authentic Italian cuisine, make Serafina a favorite with diners from around the Northwest. Serafina's philosophy is simple—offer the freshest, highest quality ingredients; present the food in an honest and inviting way; and provide the casual warmth and sultry ambiance that echo the welcoming embrace of an Italian home.

The ritual of coming together to share wine and food with family and friends is the central motif in our lives. Italian food is characterized by immediacy, honesty, and warmth: it possesses the spirit of a grandmother's wisdom and love. Italian food isn't about trailblazing alchemy or edible high fashion. Italian food is about staying connected—to each other, to the past, to the earth.

Serafina's menu recreates many of the dishes that owner Susan Kaufman and Chef John Neumark have enjoyed in friends' homes throughout Italy. The recipes we have chosen to include here are some of the most popular dishes on our menu. We encourage you to experience these recipes in the comfort of your own home as the food transports you to the gorgeous and soothing Italian countryside.

Gnocchi di Semolino

GNOCCHI
1 QT 2% MILK
1 1/2 CUPS SEMOLINA FLOUR
3 TBSP UNSALTED BUTTER
4 GREEN ONIONS, SLICED THINLY
3/4 CUP REGGIANO PARMESAN, GRATED
2 EGG YOLKS
SALT AND PEPPER TO TASTE

MUSHROOM SAUCE
1 OZ DRIED PORCINI MUSHROOMS
1 QT WATER
1 BAY LEAF

3/4 LB WILD MUSHROOMS (PREFERABLY
A MIX INCLUDING CHANTERELLES,
OYSTERS, SHITAKES)
1 LEEK, HALVED AND SLICED THINLY
INTO HALF MOONS
2 TBSP GARLIC, MINCED
1 TBSP ITALIAN PARSLEY, CHOPPED
1 TBSP FRESH THYME, CHOPPED
2 OZ MADEIRA WINE
1 TBSP IMPORTED MASCARPONE CREAM
SALT AND PEPPER
1 TBSP OLIVE OIL
1 TBSP BUTTER

SERVES 4

✤ Bring the milk to a simmer in a heavy bottomed, nonreactive pot. Slowly whisk in the semolina and continue to whisk over low heat until there are no lumps. Simmer and continue to stir for 15 minutes until mixture is very thick. Off the heat, add the butter, egg yolks, scallions, Reggiano, and salt and pepper. Mix well. Turn out onto a greased, half-sheet pan. Smooth out evenly and uniformly. Let chill thoroughly. This can be done several hours in advance.

Once the gnocchi is well chilled, cut into 1" squares.

✤ Bring mushrooms, water, and bay leaf to a boil. Simmer until reduced by half.

Heat a large 12" sauté pan over high heat. Add oil and butter and scatter the mushrooms. Do not crowd the pan (you will have to do this in batches). Toss the mushrooms well. Add leeks. Continue to toss and sauté for two minutes. Add garlic, herbs, and salt and pepper. Flame with madeira and add reduced porcini broth. Simmer gently. Check seasoning. Add mascarpone and keep warm.

Heat another large sauté pan. Add oil to coat the bottom of the pan. Add gnocchi squares. Allow to brown over medium heat. Turn and continue to brown all sides of gnocchi. Keep warm in a 350° oven until ready to serve.

Arrange 5 gnocchi per person in a large shallow bowl. Spoon sauce over to cover gnocchi and bottom of bowl. Sprinkle with grated Reggiano. Serve.

156

Zuppa di Castagne
(Chestnut Soup)

SERVES 4

Sweat leeks with butter and bay leaf over medium to low heat, covered, until softened (7 to 10 min). Add apples, chestnuts, stock, and celeriac. Bring to a boil and simmer 35 minutes. Remove bay leaf and pureé. Add heavy cream and adjust seasoning. Serve in warm bowls with a drizzle of pumpkinseed oil.

2 CUPS LEEKS, WASHED AND SLICED

1 CUP CELERIAC, PEELED AND CUBED

1 TART APPLE PEELED, CORED, AND SLICED

2-7 OZ PACKAGES OF PEELED CHESTNUTS IN CRYOVAC OR 1 1/2 QT FRESH, PEELED CHESTNUTS

3 QT CHICKEN, DUCK, OR VEGETABLE STOCK

1/2 CUP HEAVY CREAM

2 TBSP WHOLE BUTTER

1 BAY LEAF

SALT AND PEPPER TO TASTE

PUMPKINSEED OIL FOR GARNISH

157

Serafina Calamari

9 OZ SQUID, CLEANED AND SLICED
1 TBSP OLIVE OIL
2 TSP GARLIC, MINCED
1 TSP FRESH ITALIAN PARSLEY,
CHOPPED
1/2 TSP CHILI FLAKE
2 TBSP FRESH LEMON JUICE
1 TSP SALT
1 TSP BLACK PEPPER

SERVES 4

Allow a large sauté pan (12", the more surface area the better) to get astonishingly hot. Place all the ingredients in the sauté pan, EXCEPT THE LEMON JUICE. Cook, tossing frequently 20 to 30 seconds, depending on the power of your stove and the size of your sauté pan. When the squid is cooked to your liking, deglaze with lemon juice. Serve immediately.

158

Profiteroles with Bittersweet Chocolate Sauce

SERVES 4

❖ **PROFITEROLES**
1 CUP WHOLE MILK
4 OZ BUTTER
PINCH OF SALT
1 CUP ALL PURPOSE FLOUR
5 WHOLE EGGS

❖ **CHOCOLATE SAUCE**
5 OZ BITTERSWEET CHOCOLATE
1/2 CUP WATER
1/4 CUP HEAVY CREAM
1/4 CUP SUGAR

❖ Preheat oven to 350°.

Bring the milk, butter, and salt to a boil. Add the flour all at once and stir with a wooden spoon until the dough comes together. Transfer to a mixer and mix using the paddle attachment. Add the eggs, one at a time, beating until the dough is smooth and glossy. The mixture should resemble toothpaste in texture. Pipe onto a greased baking sheet and bake 15 minutes, rotating at 7 minutes.

❖ Combine all ingredients into a saucepan and warm over low heat until chocolate is melted and sauce is smooth and glossy.

ASSEMBLY

Slice the profiteroles in half along the equator and make a sandwich using your favorite ice cream as the filling. (Caramel, vanilla, milk chocolate, and coconut are our favorites.) Drizzle with warm chocolate sauce. Serve immediately.

Wine Pairing

GNOCCHI DI SEMOLINO
YAKIMA VALLEY RED WILLOW VINEYARD SANGIOVESE

ZUPPA DI CASTAGNE
COLUMBIA VALLEY MERLOT

SERAFINA CALAMARI
COLUMBIA VALLEY PINOT GRIS

PROFITEROLES WITH BITTERSWEET CHOCOLATE SAUCE
YAKIMA VALLEY OTIS VINEYARD CABERNET SAUVIGNON

DAVID LAKE, MASTER OF WINE, JOINED COLUMBIA WINERY IN 1979 as winemaker and has continued the pioneering spirit of Columbia Winery's founders. David is renowned for his experimentation with new varietals and for producing the first series of vineyard-designated wines in Washington State. He is considered the father of Washington Syrah and was the pioneer of Cabernet Franc and Pinot Gris from the region's vineyards.

Columbia Winery wines are distinctly Washington. The off-dry whites are balanced by crisp acidity and lively flavors, while the dry whites highlight bright fruit and perfectly integrated oak. The reds are rich, full-bodied wines with big tannins and a long finish. Columbia wines clearly display Lake's belief that terroir has a profound effect on the resulting wines.

Columbia Winery has a reputation for producing award-winning wines of outstanding quality and boasts a wine selection second to none. In addition to crafting excellent red wines such as Syrah, Merlot and Cabernet Sauvignon, Columbia offers distinctive dry white wines such as Chardonnay, and Pinot Gris, as well as exceptional Riesling and Gewürztraminer. Columbia Winery also offers a David Lake Signature Series of fine wines including its Cabernet Sauvignons from long-established vineyards such as Otis and the renowned Red Willow vineyard. Cabernet Franc, Merlot, Chardonnay, Sangiovese, Barbera, Zinfandel and the state's first Syrah are also part of this Signature Series.

COLUMBIA WINERY

DAVID LAKE, WINEMAKER

14030 NE 145TH STREET
WOODINVILLE, WA 98072
800.488.2347
www.columbiawinery.com

Wood Roasted Prawns, Air-dried, with Olive Oil Tomatoes, Golden Garlic and Basil

Arugula and Watercress Salad with Parmesan Crisp, Heirloom Tomato,

and Lemon Chive Vinaigrette

Pan Seared Alaskan Halibut, Fingerling Potatoes, Sautéed Pea Vines,

Kalamata Olives, and White Wine Butter

Northwest Summer Berries with Port Wine Sabayon

and Rosemary Lemonade Sorbet

Six-Seven

SIX-SEVEN RESTAURANT
IN THE EDGEWATER HOTEL
HANS REISINGER,
EXECUTIVE CHEF

PIER 67

2411 ALASKAN WAY

SEATTLE, WA 98121

206.269.4575

www.edgewaterhotel.com

THE SEA IS AT YOUR FEET, THE SUN SETS ACROSS THE WATER, THE SEALS PUT on a show, and the ferries travel to and from the islands as you watch from the best seats in Seattle—Six-Seven Restaurant in the famed Edgewater Hotel. Enter Six-Seven and you enter another world; a well-kept secret that those fortunate enough to discover, return to again and again.

Away from crowds, away from noise, a safe haven for experiencing delectable entreés such as Chef Hans Reisinger's Dungeness Crab Cakes, Alder Plank Salmon, or Red Hook Braised Short Ribs are served within the sophisticated Northwest theme of river rock fireplaces, natural wood, clean lines, and salt air. Recommended by CitySearch, "Chef Hans Reisinger keeps the menu brief and the presentation gorgeous, saving his creative energies for anomalous Asian twists on classic Northwest dishes."

Continue your experience by moving into the Six-Seven bar which boasts the same view as the restaurant and a bank of state-of-the-art video screens that provide a soothing underwater backdrop. Cap the evening off with Spanish Coffees in the lobby of the hotel before deciding whether to take the evening further by spending the night in one of the luxurious upstairs suites.

Wood Roasted Prawns, Air-dried, with Olive Oil Tomatoes, Golden Garlic and Basil

❖ MIDNIGHT TOMATOES

12 PIECES MIDNIGHT TOMATOES
1 OZ OLIVE OIL
SALT AND PEPPER TO TASTE

❖ TOMATO CONFIT

12 PIECES TOMATOE CONFIT
SALT AND PEPPER TO TASTE
SOYBEAN OIL

❖ PRAWNS

12 4-6 JUMBO PRAWNS,
PEELED AND DEVEINED
1/2 CLOVE GARLIC, CHOPPED
1 OZ SHALLOTS, CHOPPED
2 CUPS LIGHT CHICKEN STOCK
4 OZ CHILLED UNSALTED BUTTER
4 BASIL LEAVES, TORN
1 OZ BASIL, CHOPPED
PINCH OF SUGAR
6 X 8" CEDAR OR ALDER PLANK

SERVES 4

❖ Halve the tomatoes. Toss with 1 oz olive oil and salt and pepper. Place on a baking sheet or wire rack, cut side up. Dry for 4 hours at 225°.

❖ Halve the tomatoes. Toss with salt and pepper and place in a small saucepan with a cover. Fill with soybean oil until tomatoes are barely covered. Poach in 350° oven for 1 hour until tomatoes are soft. Strain out oil and set aside (excellent for salad dressings). Peel skin off tomatoes.

❖ Salt and pepper the prawns. Splash with oil. Place on cedar plank either in well-ventilated convection oven at 500° or on outside grill (the shrimp will also grill wonderfully). Sauté the shallots and garlic. Add both varieties of tomatoes and cover with the chicken stock. Let simmer 5 minutes until mixture gets thick. Top sauce with the chilled butter. Add basil and season to taste with salt and pepper. Add pinch of sugar to cut tomato's acidity.

Ladle tomatoe sauce in bottom of pasta bowl. Carefully stack prawns on top of each other. Garnish with parsley or fresh basil.

Arugula and Watercress Salad with Parmesan Crisp,
Heirloom Tomato, and Lemon Chive Vinaigrette

SERVES 4

✤ In a bowl, pour lemon juice, mustard, and vinegar. Slowly add canola oil, whisking vigorously until sauce gets thick. Cut acidity with a pinch of sugar.

✤ Cut heirloom tomatoes in quarters. Toss with olive oil. Season with salt and pepper, garlic, and basil. Let marinate for at least one half hour. Refrigerate.

✤ Preheat oven to 350°. Coarsely shred Parmesan cheese and mix with chopped parsley. Cover a greased sheet pan with parchment paper. Sprinkle cheese into a 2 1/2" circle. (Cheese should be flat. You should be able to get 8 'crisps' from the 4 oz of cheese.)

Bake on the middle rack for 5 minutes or until cheese melts and just starts to turn golden. Let cool and set aside.

✤ In a small salad bowl, combine lettuce and chives that have been cut into 1" sticks. Lightly salt and pepper the salad.

On a salad plate, place two tomatoes, 1 1/2" apart, skin side towards the rim. Place the crisps V-shaped against the tomatoes. Carefully place the salad on top of the Parmesan crisps. Serve immediately.

✤ DRESSING
4 OZ LEMON JUICE
1 OZ APPLE CIDER VINEGAR
1 TBSP DIJON MUSTARD
4 OZ CANOLA OIL

✤ TOMATOES
2 HEIRLOOM OR BEEFSTEAK TOMATOES
2 OZ OLIVE OIL
1 OZ BASIL LEAVES, TORN
1/2 OZ GARLIC, CRUSHED
SALT AND PEPPER

✤ PARMESAN CRISPS
4 OZ REGIANO PARMESAN, GRATED
1 OZ PARSLEY, CHOPPED

✤ LETTUCE
8 OZ ARUGULA, RINSED AND DRIED
8 OZ WATERCRESS, RINSED AND DRIED
2 OZ CHINESE CUT CHIVES
3 OZ LEMON CHIVE VINAIGRETTE

Pan Seared Alaskan Halibut, Fingerling Potatoes, Sautéed Pea Vines, Kalamata Olives, and White Wine Butter

❖ CHARDONNAY SAUCE
4 OZ WHITE WINE
3 OZ HEAVY CREAM
4 OZ CHILLED BUTTER

❖ FISH
4 6-7 OZ HALIBUT FILETS
2 OZ OLIVE OIL

❖ POTATOES
1 LB FINGERLING POTATOES,
PARBOILED IN HEAVILY SALTED WATER
1 LB PEA VINES
4 OZ KALAMATA OLIVES
2 OZ SHALLOTS, CHOPPED
1/2 OZ GARLIC, CHOPPED
1/2 OZ THYME, CHOPPED
1 OZ PARSLEY, CHOPPED
4 OZ OLIVE OIL
SALT, PEPPER, AND WHITE
GROUND PEPPER

SERVES 4

❖ Preheat small saucepan. Sauté 1 oz shallots. Deglaze with white wine and reduce by 50%. Add heavy cream and reduce by 50%. Slowly drop in chilled butter cubes, little by little, away from heat until sauce is thick. Season with salt and white ground pepper.

❖ In a large sauté pan, heat 2 oz olive oil until pan shows first sign of smoke. Carefully place fish skin side up and sear until golden brown. Carefully flip fish and continue to sear until fish is cooked. If fish is too thick, carefully remove the filets, set on holding plate, and place into a 300° oven until fish cooks through.

❖ In a large sauté pan, heat 2 oz olive oil until pan shows first sign of smoke. Add potatoes. Sauté until they are evenly golden brown. Add the remaining 1 oz shallots, finely chopped, the garlic, and the thyme. Sauté. Right before serving, add the pea vines and the kalamata olive. Toss in sauté pan until the pea vines show the first sign of wilting. Season with salt and pepper. Serve immediately.

ASSEMBLY
Carefully arrange the potatoes on the center of the plate, topping off with the wilted pea vines and kalamata olives. Place the cooked Alaskan halibut on top of the potatoes. Ladle the sauce over the fish. Garnish with chopped parsley.

166

Northwest Summer Berries with Port Wine Sabayon and Rosemary Lemonade Sorbet

SERVES 4

Place berries in bowl and gently toss with the 2 tbsp of sugar. Set aside.

Set up a double boiler on the stove. In mixing bowl, put the egg yolks, sugar, port wine, and white wine. Set the bowl over the pot of steaming water. Whisk vigorously for 4 to 6 minutes until the mixture gets thick and you no longer see the air bubbles in the mixture.

Evenly divide the berries in a large martini glass. Top off with a scoop of sorbet. Carefully ladle the Sabayon over the sorbet. Garnish with a fresh mint sprig. Serve immediately.

1 PINT RASPBERRIES
1 PINT BLACKBERRIES
1 PINT BLUEBERRIES
2 TBSP SUGAR
4 EGG YOLKS
4 OZ GRANULATED SUGAR
4 OZ SIX-GRAPE PORT WINE
2 OZ WHITE WINE
1 PINT ROSEMARY LEMONADE SORBET
(OR YOUR FAVORITE FLAVOR)
MINT FOR GARNISH

Wine Pairing

Wood Roasted Prawns, Air-dried, with Olive Oil Tomatoes,
Golden Garlic and Basil

Arugula and Watercress Salad with Parmesan Crisp,
Heirloom Tomato, and Lemon Chive Vinaigrette

Pan Seared Alaskan Halibut, Fingerling Potatoes,
Sautéed Pea Vines, Kalamata Olives,
and White Wine Butter

Northwest Summer Berries with Port Wine Sabayon and
Rosemary Lemonade Sorbet

Quilceda Creek Cabernet Sauvignon

QUILCEDA CREEK

VINTNERS

ALEX GOLITZIN WAS BORN IN FRANCE AT THE BEGINNING OF WORLD WAR II and lived in Paris for the duration of the war. In 1946, his family immigrated to California. They settled in San Francisco, close to the Napa Valley where his uncle, Andre Tchelistcheff, was winemaker at Beaulieu Vineyards.

Jeannette Golitzin was brought up in San Francisco by paternal grandparents from France. Everything in their household revolved around France including language, traditions, winemaking, and exquisite French cooking. Alex and Jeannette were high school sweethearts and married in 1963.

In 1974, with Uncle Andre's help, Alex made his first barrel of Cabernet. Following three more vintages and three more barrels, Alex and Jeannette bonded the winery in 1978 and produced the first Quilceda Creek Cabernet in 1979. Four years later, this wine received a Gold Medal and a Grand Prize at the Enological Society Festival in Seattle.

Together with their son Paul and sons-in-law Marv Crum and John Ware, the Golitzins and Quilceda Creek continue to pursue the quest for the ultimate Cabernet.

"Quilceda Creek's saturated black-colored 2001 Cabernet Sauvignon continues this winery's brilliant string of successes. Its intense aromas reveal a huge depth of blackberry and cassis fruit. Concentrated, backward, and deep, it is a medium to full-bodied wine with exceptional balance, purity, focus, and length. Powerful yet refined, it coats the palate with cassis and jammy blackberries whose flavors linger for almost a minute." Pierre-Antoine Rovani, Robert M. Parker Jr.'s, *The Wine Advocate*

"Is there a winery in the world that has produced a finer set of Cabernet over the past decade?" Robert M. Parker Jr., *The Wine Advocate*

THE GOLITZIN FAMILY,
OWNERS

PO BOX 1562

SNOHOMISH, WA 98291

360.568.2389

www.quilcedacreek.com

Hot Smoked Salmon Appetizer

SkyCity Salad, Pressed Sushi Rice

Grilled Pork Chops with Maker's Mark Glaze

Sky City Berry Pie

SkyCity at the Space Needle

SKYCITY AT THE SPACE NEEDLE
GERARD BENGLE,
EXECUTIVE CHEF

400 BROAD STREET

SEATTLE, WA 98109

206.905.2100

www.spaceneedle.com

SKYCITY IS A ROOM WITH A VIEW. ACTUALLY, IT'S A REVOLVING ROOM with *the* view of Seattle, Puget Sound, and the mountains. SkyCity is a restaurant that floats 500 feet in the air, spinning gracefully on a turntable atop Seattle's Space Needle.

The food rivals the stunning 360-degree view. Chef Gerard Bengle's menu includes seared ahi tuna with wasabi mashed potatoes, tender prime rib, and scallops in champagne sauce. SkyCity has a prix fixe weekend brunch full of tempting choices, from prawn omelets to Belgian waffles to oyster shooters. The restaurant excels in the details, including the distinctive (and delicious) use of hazelnut oil for dipping bread, a wine list that allows the diner to choose a wine by the glass from among many of the listed bottled wines, and a playful ice cream dessert called the Lunar Orbiter that resembles the Space Needle on a mysterious foggy night. The restaurant has been recently remodeled into elegant '60s chic with a hint of Asian influence.

SkyCity is the obvious choice to watch a beautiful summer sunset or to enjoy an enchanting romantic night viewing the city lights and the moon and the stars. The restaurant is also an excellent choice for a business lunch to impress an out-of-town colleague. Since the ride up the elevator and use of the Observation Deck of the Space Needle is free when you dine at SkyCity, it's worth taking the extra time for a stroll at the top of the world.

Hot Smoked Salmon Appetizer

❖ SMOKED SALMON
MARINADE
3/4 CUP BROWN SUGAR
1/4 CUP KOSHER SALT
2 TBSP HONEY
1 TBSP SHERRY
1 TBSP WATER
2 TBSP GARLIC, MINCED
DASH WORCESTERSHIRE SAUCE
DASH TABASCO SAUCE

3 LBS OF BONELESS, SKINLESS SALMON

RICE CAKES
CLARIFIED BUTTER FOR SEARING

❖ APPLE SALSA
2 LARGE BRAEBURN OR FUJI APPLES
1 WALLA WALLA SWEET ONION OR
OTHER TYPE OF SWEET ONION
1 RED BELL PEPPER
1 BUNCH CILANTRO
APPLE VINAIGRETTE TO COAT

❖ APPLE VINAIGRETTE
3/4 CUP CIDER VINEGAR
1/4 CUP APPLE JUICE
1/8 CUP PARSLEY, MINCED
3/4 CUP HONEY
1 TBSP KOSHER SALT
1 TSP WHITE PEPPER
1 SHALLOT, MINCED
2 3/4 CUP CANOLA OIL

SERVES 4

❖ Place all ingredients in a bowl. Mix well and add approximately 3 lbs of boneless, skinless salmon. Cut into the portion size you desire. Allow salmon to marinate in the refrigerator overnight.

The following day, heat up the smoker. Place the salmon on racks and smoke on low heat for 20 minutes. Remove salmon from the smoker and place in a 300° oven for 15 to 20 minutes. Remove when done.

❖ Juilenne the apples, onion, and red bell pepper. Toss with apple vinaigrette. Chop cilantro and add to mixture.

❖ Combine first 7 ingredients. Whisk in the canola oil. Cover and chill.

ASSEMBLY

As the salmon is finishing in the oven, pan sear rice cakes with clarified butter in a hot sauce pan. Place the pan-seared rice cake on individual plates. Put a small mound of apple salsa in front of the rice cake and top with the smoked salmon. Garnish with green onions or fresh pea sprouts.

172

Sky City Salad

SERVES 4

4 OZ BLUE VEIN CHEESE,
CUT INTO 1 OZ SLICES

12 OZ FIELD GREENS

4 OZ HUCKLEBERRY DRESSING

1 BARTLETT PEAR

Core and slice pear into 16 slices. Arrange pear on individual plates, 4 slices to a plate. Toss greens with dressing. Place mixed greens in the center of each plate and garnish with cheese slice in the center of the pears, leaning into salad.

Huckleberry Dressing

SERVES 4-8

1 CUP HUCKLEBERRIES

1/2 CUP SUGAR

1 QUART APPLE HONEY DRESSING

Combine all ingredients. Do not machine mix, whip by hand.

❖ APPLE HONEY DRESSING

1 CUP CIDER VINEGAR

1/2 CUP APPLE JUICE

1/2 CUP HONEY

1/4 CUP PARSLEY, FINELY CHOPPED

1 TBSP SHALLOTS, MINCED

3 CUPS VEGETABLE OIL

❖ Combine all ingredients (except for the vegetable oil) into a blender and mix at low speed. Add the vegetable oil to the mixture 1 cup at a time.

Pressed Sushi Rice

SERVES 4

1 CUP NIKKO RICE

1 1/4 CUP WARM WATER

1/2 CUP RICE WINE VINEGAR

1/4 CUP SUGAR

1/2 TSP KOSHER SALT

Combine warm water and sugar. Stir until dissolved. Add remainder of ingredients. Pour into a saucepan and cover with parchment and foil. Bake at 350° for 30 to 40 minutes. Transfer rice onto a baking sheet. Form into a block. Cover with parchment paper and roll into a roll. Chill overnight. Before serving, cut the rice with a sharp knife dipped in water.

Grilled Pork Chops with Maker's Mark Glaze

4 EACH 14 OZ DOUBLE BONE-IN PORK
CHOPS (ASK THE BUTCHER TO "FRENCH"
THE BONES FOR YOU.)

❖ BRINE
1 TBSP SALT
1 QT WATER

❖ MAKER'S MARK GLAZE
3/4 CUP MAKER'S MARK BOURBON
1 CUP CHICKEN STOCK
1/3 CUP REAL MAPLE SYRUP
2 TSP CORNSTARCH MIXED WITH 2 TBSP
COLD WATER

PORK CHOP MARINADE
1 BRAEBURN APPLE, PEELED AND SEEDED
1/4 CUP ONION, DICED
2 CLOVES GARLIC, MINCED
1/4 CUP BALSAMIC VINEGAR
1/8 CUP OLIVE OIL
1/4 CUP BROWN SUGAR

SERVES 4

❖ Mix the salt and water. Soak pork chops overnight. This pre-seasons the pork and adds moisture to the final product.

❖ Pour Maker's Mark Bourbon into a 3 qt saucepan and place on a burner set at medium heat. Carefully ignite the alcohol, being very careful, as there is a significant amount of alcohol to burn off. After the flames burn out, add the chicken stock and maple syrup. Thicken with the cornstarch mixture.

Either start the pork chops atop a broiler or sear in a sauté pan. Place in a 350° oven until the internal temperature reaches 165° on a meat thermometer (approximately 25 minutes). Remove the pork chops from the oven and allow to rest for 5 minutes.

Assemble on individual plates with the accompaniment of your choice.

174

Sky City Berry Pie

SERVES 2

❖ In a large bowl, mix the butter, flour, vegetable shortening and salt until the mixture is course, like meal. Add 2 tbsp of ice water to the mixture until the water is incorporated. Add more ice water, if needed, to form a dough. Form the dough into a ball. Dust the dough with flour. Wrap the dough in wax paper and chill for 1 hour.

Roll out half the dough 1/8" thick on a lightly floured surface, fit it into a 9" deep-dish pie plate. Trim the edge, leaving a 1/2"overhang. Chill the shell while making the filling.

❖ In a large bowl, toss together the berries, cornstarch, 1 1/2 cups of sugar, lemon juice, nutmeg, and cinnamon until the mixture is combined well. Mound the filling in the shell. Dot with the butter bits.

Bake the pie on a large baking sheet in the middle of a preheated 425° oven for 20 minutes. Reduce the heat to 375°. Bake the pie for 35 to 40 additional minutes or until the crust is golden and the filling is bubbling. Serve the pie with ice cream while it is still warm.

❖ PASTRY

1 1/2 CUPS ALL-PURPOSE FLOUR

2 TBSP COLD VEGETABLE SHORTENING

3/4 STICK COLD UNSALTED BUTTER, CUT INTO SMALL PIECES

1/4 TSP OF SALT

❖ FILLING

3 CUPS FRESH BLACKBERRIES

3 CUPS FRESH BLUEBERRIES

2 1/2 CUPS FRESH RASPBERRIES (PAT ALL BERRIES TO DRY)

1/2 CUP CORNSTARCH

1 1/2 CUPS SUGAR PLUS ADDITIONAL TO SPRINKLE ON THE PIE

1/4 CUP FRESH LEMON JUICE

1/8 TSP GRATED NUTMEG

1/8 TSP CINNAMON

1 TBSP UNSALTED BUTTER, CUT INTO SMALL PIECES

Wine Pairing

HOT SMOKED SALMON APPETIZER
COLUMBIA VALLEY SAUVIGNON BLANC OR
COLUMBIA VALLEY CHENIN BLANC

SKYCITY SALAD, PRESSED SUSHI RICE
COLUMBIA VALLEY CHARDONNAY

GRILLED PORK CHOPS WITH MAKER'S MARK GLAZE,
PRESSED SUSHI RICE
RESERVE SYRAH

SKY CITY BERRY PIE
WINEMAKER'S SELECT RIESLING

SYRAH

Columbia Valley

SNOQUALMIE
VINEYARDS

STE. MICHELLE
WINE ESTATES,
OWNER

660 FRONTIER ROAD

PROSSER, WA 99350

800.852.0885

www.snoqualmie.com

THE PACIFIC NORTHWEST IS FAMOUS FOR ITS NATURAL BEAUTY— towering evergreens and snow-capped Cascade Mountains. Snoqualmie Vineyards (sno kwal' me) takes its name from the rugged mountain pass at the top of the Cascade range that serves as the entryway to Eastern Washington and the Columbia and Yakima valleys. Here the skies are sunny and the climate is dry—perfect conditions for growing world-class grapes.

It is in the small town of Prosser, the "Gateway to Washington Wine Country," where visitors will find Snoqualmie Vineyards. Under the leadership of Winemaker Joy Andersen, Snoqualmie has been producing award-winning wines for over two decades. Snoqualmie's reputation for releasing approachable, food-friendly wines has been recognized across the country by critics and consumers alike. Joy's approach to winemaking is to pull the simple fruit flavors out of the grapes to create distinctive wines with bright, bold tastes. Snoqualmie is best known for its award winning Reserve Merlot and Cabernet Sauvignon, Syrah, Cabernet-Merlot, and Chenin Blanc.

TUNA TARTARE APPETIZER

SCALLOPS WITH PORCINI BROTH AND VEGETABLE RAGOUT

HALIBUT CEVICHE

OVEN ROASTED PEACHES AND LEMON THYME CREAM IN AN ALMOND MERINGUE SHELL

Third Floor Fish Café

THIRD FLOOR FISH CAFE
GREG CAMPBELL,
EXECUTIVE CHEF

205 LAKE STREET S

KIRKLAND, WA 98033

425.822.3553

www.fishcafe.com

FOR THE PAST TWO YEARS, THE THIRD FLOOR FISH CAFÉ, HAS BEEN THE MOST award-winning restaurant on Seattle's Eastside. Located in the shoreline town of Kirkland and sitting atop the third floor waterside establishment, you enjoy your meal while feasting your eyes on beautiful Lake Washington and the Seattle skyline. As reviewer Sue Kidd noted, "It's hard to believe, but the menu actually outshines the view."

That's because the restaurant boosts the culinary expertise of Executive Chef Greg Campbell, Culinary Institute of America alum and former member of Wolfgang Puck's enterprise. Enjoy Chef Campbell's Copper River salmon with an intriguing mélange of fennel and red onions splashed with tomato vinaigrette and topped with fresh cod and rock shrimp. Or pique your tastebuds with pan-seared wild sturgeon with a shitake mushroom vinaigrette sitting atop a crunchy rice cake. Add other menu items such as the Peppercorn Crusted Ahi, the Seafood Paella, or steamed clams in a rich bourbon-laced sauce with bits of sausage and a hint of fennel and you'll think you've died and gone to seafood heaven. Cap your meal with any one of the mouth watering desserts The Third Floor Fish Café offers, including the white chocolate mousse served with fresh raspberries and raspberry sauce.

Complete your evening listening to the sounds of piano player Tim Kruse before you head out to walk Lake Washington Boulevard. There you'll bask in the sights and sounds of the lakeshore, and the shops and the atmosphere of the town of Kirkland—Washington's own version of Carmel.

Tuna Tartare Appetizer

❖ TUNA

1 1/2 LB SUSHI GRADE TUNA,
CUT INTO 1/4" DICE
1/4 CUP BLACK AND WHITE
SESAME SEEDS, TOASTED
2 SCALLIONS, GREEN PART ONLY,
SLICED THIN
1 TBSP WASABI
2 TBSP SOY SAUCE

SERVES 4

❖ Mix the wasabi and soy sauce together until smooth. Add the other ingredients and mix. Do this immediately before serving to maintain the color of the tuna

❖ Mix all together. Season with salt and pepper. Add additional wasabi to taste.

❖ WASABI OBA AIOLI

1 TBSP WASABI
1 EGG YOLK
1/4 CUP RICE WINE VINEGAR
3 TBSP FRESH LIME JUICE
2 TBSP PICKLED GINGER, CHOPPED
1/2 BUNCH CILANTRO,
PICKED AND CHOPPED
1 BUNCH MINT
2 TBSP HONEY
1/2 CUP GRAPE SEED OIL
SALT AND PEPPER

Halibut Ceviche

SERVES 4

Dice the halibut into 1/4" or smaller pieces. Cover with fresh lime juice. Season with salt and pepper. Marinate for at least 4 hours or overnight, if possible. When fish is done marinating, drain excess juice and toss with red onion, cilantro, jalapeño, and diced avocado. Adjust the seasoning. Serve with tortilla chips.

11/2 LB FRESH HALIBUT FILET,
SKIN REMOVED
JUICE OF 4 LIMES
1/2 BUNCH CILANTRO, MINCED
1/2 RED ONION, MINCED
1/2 JALAPEÑO, MINCED
3 ROMA TOMATOES, SEEDED AND DICED
1 AVOCADO, DICED

Scallops with Porcini Broth and Vegetable Ragout

SERVES 4

❖ In a stockpot, melt 1/4 lb of butter and sauté all ingredients until soft. Cover the vegetables with cold water. Bring to a boil. After the stock boils, turn it off. Let steep for 20 minutes. Strain the stock and blend in the rest of the butter. Season with salt and pepper

❖ The key to good ragout is to par-cook all of the vegetables individually so that when you are ready to serve the dish they just need to be quickly sautéed.

❖ BROTH
1 LB CRIMINI MUSHROOM STEMS
2 CARROTS, CHOPPED
1 YELLOW ONION, SLICED
5 CLOVES GARLIC, SLICED
3 SHALLOTS, SLICED
1 BUNCH THYME
1 HANDFUL OF DRIED PORCINI
MUSHROOMS (OPTIONAL)
1/2 LB BUTTER
SALT AND PEPPER

❖ RAGOUT
(THE RAGOUT FOR THIS DISH
SHOULD BE MADE USING THE
FRESHEST VEGETABLES AVAILABLE.)
1/2 LB BABY CARROTS,
PEELED AND BLANCHED
1/2 LB FRENCH BEANS, BLANCHED
1 HEAD OF ROASTED GARLIC
12 ROASTED SHALLOTS
12 CHERRY TOMATOES, STEMS OFF
1/2 LB CRIMINI MUSHROOMS,
QUARTERED AND SAUTÉED

Oven Roasted Peaches and Lemon Thyme Cream in an Almond Meringue Shell

✤ ALMOND MERINGUE SHELLS

SERVES 8

4 LARGE EGG WHITES
1/4 TSP CREAM OF TARTAR
1/8 TSP SALT
3/4 CUP SUGAR
1 TSP VANILLA EXTRACT
1/2 CUP SLICED ALMONDS

✤ ROASTED PEACHES

6 LARGE RIPE PEACHES
1/3 CUP LIGHT BROWN SUGAR
1/2 CUP GRANULATED SUGAR
1/2 CINNAMON STICK
4 WHOLE CLOVES
2 OZ FRESH ORANGE JUICE
2 OZ FRESH LEMON JUICE
4 3" SPRIGS FRESH LEMON THYME

✤ LEMON THYME PASTRY CREAM

2 CUPS WHOLE MILK
4 3" SPRIGS FRESH LEMON THYME
ZEST FROM 1 LEMON, FINELY CHOPPED
6 EGG YOLKS FROM LARGE EGGS
1/2 CUP SUGAR
1/4 TSP SALT
2 TBSP FLOUR
1/2 CUP HEAVY WHIPPING CREAM
1/2 TSP VANILLA EXTRACT

✤ Preheat oven to 200°.

Line two baking pans with parchment paper. Whip egg whites, cream of tartar, and salt on medium speed until egg whites begin to thicken. Increase speed and gradually add sugar. Whip to soft peak. Add vanilla extract and whip to firm peak.

Drop the meringue onto the baking sheets in 4 even mounds per baking sheet. Use a soup spoon dipped in cool water to make each meringue mound into a shallow bowl. Gently press the almonds around the outside of each meringue. Bake for 2 hours. Turn off the oven. Leave the shells in the oven for an additional hour.

✤ Preheat oven to 350°.

Blanch the peaches in boiling water for 30 seconds to 1 minute. Immediately place in ice water. The peel should slip off easily. Slice each peach into 12 slices. Place in an ovenproof baking dish. Set aside.

Place all remaining ingredients in a saucepan. Bring to a low boil. Cook for 4 to 5 minutes. Pour the hot syrup over the peaches. Cover the dish with foil. Bake in the oven for 15 minutes. Remove from the oven and remove the foil.

Let the peaches cool to room temperature in the syrup. Remove the peaches from the syrup. Strain the syrup through a strainer. Pour back over the peaches until ready to use.

✤ Place the milk, lemon thyme, and lemon zest in a saucepan. Heat to scalding over medium heat. Remove from the heat. Cover and let sit for 30 minutes.

Whisk the egg yolks, sugar, and salt together until pale yellow. Whisk in the flour until completely smooth. Slowly temper the egg yolks with the hot milk. Return to the heat and cook over medium heat, whisking constantly until the mixture comes to a low boil. Cook for an additional 2 minutes.

Strain through a fine mesh strainer into a bowl. Cover the surface with plastic wrap and chill in the refrigerator until completely cold. Just before you are ready to assemble the dessert, whip the cream and vanilla to soft peak. Fold into the cold pastry cream in three additions.

ASSEMBLY

Fill each almond meringue shell 3/4 of the way full with the lemon thyme pastry cream. Fill the rest of the way with the roasted peaches. Garnish the plate with the remaining peaches, fresh berries, and sprigs of fresh lemon thyme.

Wine Pairing

Tuna Tartare Appetizer
2000 Apex Dry Riesling
Columbia Valley

Halibut Ceviche
2001 Apex Chardonnay Outlook Vineyard
Yakima Valley

Scallops with Porcini Broth and Vegetable Ragout
2000 Apex Syrah
Yakima Valley

Oven Roasted Peaches and Lemon Thyme Cream
in an Almond Meringue Shell
2003 Apex Gewurztraminer Ice Wine
Yakima Valley

VINTAGE 2000

APEX

YAKIMA VALLEY

Syrah

ALCOHOL 14.4% BY VOLUME

APEX

CELLARS

HARRY ALHADEFF,
OWNER
BRIAN CARTER,
WINEMAKER

111 E LINCOLN AVENUE

SUNNYSIDE, WA 98944

800.814.7004

www.apexcellars.com

IN 1988, HARRY ALHADEFF, ONE OF THE NORTHWEST'S MOST KNOWLEDGEABLE wine retailers and distributors, and Brian Carter, a winemaker of extraordinary depth and experience, launched Apex Cellars. Brian is one of the pioneers of the modern Washington wine industry. 2004 marks his 25th harvest in the Columbia and Yakima Valleys. His mastery of his craft is shown in the countless awards and accolades he has earned and in the delicious wines he turns out year after year.

The combination of Harry's knowledge and experience in the wine business and Brian's uncanny ability to combine the science and art of winemaking results in extraordinary wines and extraordinary success. Apex Cellars has one of the state's most enviable records for awards per wine entered in local, regional and national competitions. All of the winery's brands have received glowing reviews from respected wine experts here and abroad.

Brian has twice been recognized as Winemaker of the Year and is the only three-time winner of the Pacific Northwest Enological Society's prestigious and rarely given Grand Award.

The wines are recognized everywhere for their harmony and grace, balance and supple texture. The Apex style reflects wines of depth, concentration, and unusual complexity that make for wines that are beautifully easy to drink and the perfect accompaniment to any occasion.

Fresh Scallops with Orange Sweet Pepper Sauce

Basil Cured Tuna with Potato Caponata

Filet of Beef with Truffle Cream and Braised Pancetta

Chocolate Hazelnut Semifreddo with Orange Reduction

Troiani

TROIANI

BUCKY JAMES
CHEF

DEMO NICAS
CHEF

RICH TROIANI
OWNER/HOST

PAUL MACKAY
OWNER

1001 THIRD AVENUE

SEATTLE, WA 98104

206.624.4060

www.troianiseattle.com

TROIANI HAS APTLY DESCRIBED ITSELF AS "AN UPSCALE ITALIAN GRILL." Troiani resides in a handsomely modern and vast dining room in the middle of Seattle's downtown business district, with broad windows and an open kitchen. The restaurant has high, wood ceilings, expansive and comfortable booths, and a popular after-work bar.

Troiani presents a menu that offers calamari on a mint, tomato, and avocado salad; charcoal grilled escarole salad with pancetta; half Maine lobster fettucini; crispy duck breast; and the restaurant's signature entrée, Steak Troiani (a tenderloin of New York for two). Desserts are Troiani's irresistible versions of Italian classics including gelato, cannoli, chocolate semifreddo, and Granita, Moscato di Asti with summer berries and lemon cream. The wine list is extensive and naturally favors Italian wines. (Troiani also has an impressive single malt scotch list.) The restaurant has a noticeably friendly, unpretentious staff.

Troiani opened in December 2003 and was featured in *The New York Times* just four months later. It has quickly earned positive reviews from all of the local newspapers. The restaurant is named after one of the co-founders, Rich Troiani.

Fresh Scallops with Orange Sweet Pepper Sauce

❖ ORANGE PEPPER SAUCE

2 ORANGE PEPPERS,
SMALL DICE NOT PEELED
2 ORANGE PEPPERS, SMALL DICE,
ROASTED AND PEELED
4 SHALLOTS, ROASTED
4 OZ GOLDEN RAISINS
1 CUP VIRGIN OLIVE OIL
KOSHER SALT AND WHITE PEPPER,

❖ SCALLOPS

20 MEDIUM FRESH SCALLOPS
1 CUP VIRGIN OLIVE OIL
KOSHER SALT AND FRESH BLACK PEPPER

SERVES 4

❖ In a heavy bottom saucepot, begin to sauté both peppers, shallots, and raisins in olive oil. Don't brown the peppers. Cook until peppers are soft. Cover the pot. Turn to a very low heat for 20 minutes. The peppers should be soft and the juices are released. Place in a blender and blend until the mixture is very smooth. Season with white pepper and kosher salt. Set aside at room temperature.

❖ Season the scallops with kosher salt and fresh black pepper. In a heavy bottom sauté pan, heat the olive oil. When the pan begins to smoke, place the scallops in the pan. Sear the scallops on both sides for approximately 2 minutes or until the scallops have a nice brown color on both sides. Try to turn the scallops only once during this process. You should be able to complete this entire process on top of the stove. Scallops should be slightly undercooked to avoid toughness or drying out.

Drain the scallops on a paper towel and place on a warm plate. Garnish each scallop with Orange Pepper Sauce. A great accompaniment is couscous with fresh herbs and golden raisins or sautéed spinach with olive oil, pine nuts, and golden raisins.

188

Basil Cured Tuna with Potato Caponata

SERVES 4

Mix together kosher salt, brown sugar, and fresh basil. Lay the cheesecloth on a board and place a bed of the curing mixture on the cheesecloth the length of the tuna. Place the tuna on top of the mixture. Add the remaining mixture to the top and sides. The tuna needs to be covered. Begin to roll the cheesecloth over the tuna until it is completely wrapped in the cloth and encased in the salt mixture. Place in a pan and into the refrigerator for 6 to 7 hours.

Start prepping the potato caponota. In a saucepot of boiling salted water, blanch the diced potatoes for approximately 5 minutes or until potatoes are tender, but still a little firm. Carefully drain the potatoes and cool in the refrigerator.

In a saucepan, heat olive oil and add the diced peppers and onions. Sauté slowly until soft. Add the blanched diced potatoes. Toss for 30 seconds. Remove from heat. Add chopped basil, parsley, salt, fresh black pepper, and more virgin olive oil. Set aside at room temperature.

After the tuna has cured, wash the curing mixture under cold running water then dry thoroughly.

ASSEMBLY

Place a bed of the caponata on the platter. Using a very sharp knife, slice the tuna into 1/8" slices. Place the sliced tuna on the caponota and garnish with Nicoise olives.

1 LB FRESH AHI TUNA, SLICED INTO 12"X 2" PIECES
1 LB FRESH BASIL LEAVES (LEAVES ONLY, NO STEMS), CHOPPED (3/4 LB FOR CURING AND 1/4 LB FOR CAPONATA)
1/4 LB ITALIAN PARSLEY, CHOPPED
1 CUP BROWN SUGAR
2 CUPS KOSHER SALT
1/4 CUP NICOISE OLIVES (OR ANY SMALL OLIVE)
4 YUKON GOLD POTATOES, PEELED AND CUT 1/8" SQUARES
2 WHITE ONIONS, CUT INTO 1/8" SQUARE PIECES
2 RED PEPPERS CUT INTO 1/8" SQUARE PIECES
VIRGIN OLIVE OIL
4"X 16" PIECE OF CHEESECLOTH

189

Filet of Beef with Truffle Cream and Braised Pancetta

4 8 OZ FILET MIGNON

KOSHER SALT TO TASTE

1 TSP FRESH BLACK PEPPER

OLIVE OIL

❖ BRAISED PANCETTA

1 LB PANCETTA, WHOLE PIECE

6 CUPS CHICKEN STOCK

2 EACH CELERY, CARROTS, ONIONS, AND

LEEKS, SMALL DICE AND WASHED

❖ TRUFFLE CREAM

1 OZ WHITE TRUFFLE OIL

1 OZ BLACK PEPPER, COURSE

AND BLANCHED

1/2 CUP WHIPPING CREAM

SERVES 4

❖ In a heavy bottom saucepot, begin to heat the pan. Add the seasoned pancetta piece. Brown well on both sides, approximately 15 minutes. Remove the pancetta from the pan. Add diced vegetables. Sauté until soft. Place the browned pancetta on the sautéed vegetables and add 3 cups chicken stock. Cover. Place in 350° oven for 1 hour. Check after 1 hour. Add another 2 cups of chicken stock. Return to the oven for 1 more hour or until pancetta is very tender. Remove and cool. Score across the fat. Slice into 1/8" slices and reheat in a 400° oven.

❖ Whip the whipping cream into light peaks. Fold in truffle oil, blanched black pepper, salt and pepper.

Preheat the oven to 375°.

Season the filet of beef well with kosher salt and fresh black pepper. Heat olive oil in a heavy bottom saucepan until the pan begins to slightly smoke. Add the seasoned beef to the pan. Sear on each side for approximately 2 minutes or until the beef has a nice color. Place the pan into the oven. Roast the meat for approximately 10 minutes for medium rare. If you require it more well done, add an additional 5 to 7 minutes for each degree of doneness. Turn the filet during the cooking process.

Remove the meat from the oven and let rest for a few minutes. Place the meat on the plate and garnish with 3 slices of the warm, braised pancetta on the side. Finish the beef with a generous dollop of the truffle cream on top of the filet. A great accompaniment is rosemary-roasted potatoes or whipped potatoes with ricotta cheese.

190

Chocolate Hazelnut Semifreddo with Orange Reduction

Prepare at least eight hours before serving.

SERVES 6

❖ ORANGE REDUCTION
1 QUART ORANGE JUICE

❖ Bring the juice to a simmer. Skim any foam off the top of the liquid. Reduce until it is syrup consistency and coats the back of a spoon. This may take up to, and over, an hour. Refrigerate.

❖ CHOCOLATE HAZELNUT SEMIFREDDO
1 CUP HAZELNUTS, TOASTED, WITH SKINS GENTLY RUBBED OFF AND ROUGHLY CHOPPED
8 OZ DARK CHOCOLATE
2 TBSP BUTTER

❖ Prepare hazelnuts. Melt chocolate and butter separately. Let them cool slightly.

❖ ITALIAN MERINGUE
5 EGG WHITES
1 CUP OF SUGAR
1 1/4 CUPS HEAVY CREAM

❖ Mix egg whites and sugar. Place in a double boiler. Stir occasionally while heating to 150 °. Place in a mixer bowl and whisk until stiff peaks form. Whip heavy cream to soft peaks.

Mix together hazelnuts and butter. Quickly fold together hazelnut mixture and chocolate. Fold the Italian meringue into the chocolate mixture in 3 additions. Finally, fold the whipped cream into the chocolate/meringue mixture in 3 additions.

Line a loaf pan with plastic wrap or parchment. Fill it with the mixture. Freeze for at least 8 hours or overnight.

ASSEMBLY
Cut a 1" slice of semifreddo and place it in the center of the plate. Spoon a generous circle of orange reduction around the plate.

Wine Pairing

FRESH SCALLOPS WITH ORANGE SWEET PEPPER SAUCE
COLUMBIA VALLEY SÉMILLON & SAUVIGNON BLANC

BASIL CURED TUNA WITH POTATO CAPONATA
COLUMBIA VALLEY CONNER LEE VINEYARD CHARDONNAY

FILET OF BEEF WITH TRUFFLE CREAM AND BRAISED PANCETTA
COLUMBIA VALLEY MERLOT & CABERNET FRANC

CHOCOLATE HAZELNUT SEMIFREDDO WITH ORANGE REDUCTION
WALLA WALLA VALLEY REDIVIVA OF THE STONES

buty
2002
COLUMBIA VALLEY

Conner Lee Vineyard
CHARDONNAY

ALCOHOL 13.8% BY VOLUME

BUTY

WINERY

CALEB FOSTER AND
NINA BUTY FOSTER,
OWNERS

535 E CESSNA AVENUE

WALLA WALLA, WA 99362

509.527.0901

www.butywinery.com

BUTY IS NINA BUTY FOSTER AND CALEB FOSTER'S FAMILY MICRO-WINERY in Walla Walla. Established in 2000, Buty wines reflect experience developed from Caleb's eight-year apprenticeship at Woodward Canyon Winery and his experience in overseas winemaking in New Zealand and South Africa. To grow character in the wines, Buty focuses its winemaking efforts in the vineyard, and offers small cuvées of terroir-driven wines grown with balanced yields and high ripeness.

Buty was first recognized for producing classical vineyard-designated Chardonnay with pronounced fruit and site expression. In addition, Buty creates the traditional blends of Sémillon and Sauvignon Blanc, and Merlot and Cabernet Franc. These wines are purely about expressive Washington aromas and flavors.

The Northwest's new classic comes from Buty. Rediviva is the marriage of Cabernet Sauvignon's intensity and Syrah's complexity. Rediviva of the Stones, which favors Syrah, is grown in the ancestral Walla Walla riverbed cobblestones. Columbia Rediviva is grown in the Horse Heaven Hills and is dominated by Cabernet Sauvignon.

With their lives tied to the seasons, Nina and Caleb enjoy creatively shaping Buty for exceptional winegrowing and winemaking.

Wicked Shrimp

Seasonal Greens with Spiced Pecans, Gorgonzola, and Sherry Vinaigrette

Ahi Piccata

Waterfront Chocolate Cake

Waterfront

WATERFRONT SEAFOOD GRILL
PAUL MACKAY,
OWNER
STEVE CAIN,
EXECUTIVE CHEF
CHRISTIAN SPARKMAN,
GENERAL MANAGER

GEORGEOUS AND WARMLY ELEGANT, THE WATERFRONT SEAFOOD GRILL, Seattle's hidden jewel, sparkles at the tip of Pier 70. Walls of glass frame 270° views of Elliott Bay, Magnolia Bluff, and the Space Needle. The warm décor offers the perfect environment to pass those winter months. And nowhere is there a more perfect setting to enjoy Seattle's summer evenings than the amazing deck at the end of the pier.

Waterfront's winter menu features fresh seafood preparations with a hint of nostalgia. Fresh daily selections of fish and certified Angus prime beef are prepared on an open-pit charcoal grill in the exhibition kitchen. The lobster mashed potatoes are epic; the rack of lamb addictive. The Baked Alaska provides a fiery climax to an extraordinary evening of culinary delight and excellent service. Take in the view while sipping a Cloudy Day cocktail at the remarkable lighted wave bar as it changes hues of marine blue. Linger by the piano for jazzy renditions of old favorites. Satisfy your need for the sea, delicious food, and beautiful atmosphere as you make Waterfront Seafood Grill one of your favorites.

2801 ALASKAN WAY, PIER 70

SEATTLE, WA 98121

206.956.9171

www.waterfrontpier70.com

Wicked Shrimp

❖ SPICE MIXTURE

1/2 TBSP CAYENNE PEPPER
1/2 TBSP GROUND BLACK PEPPER
1 TSP KOSHER SALT
1 TSP CRUSHED RED PEPPER
(CHILI FLAKES)
1 TSP DRIED THYME
1 TSP DRIED ROSEMARY
1 TSP OREGANO

❖ REMAINING INGREDIENTS

1 LB PRAWNS
1/4 LB SOFTENED BUTTER
1 1/2 TSP GARLIC, MINCED
1 1/2 TSP WORCESTERSHIRE SAUCE
1/2 CUP BEER (ALE)
1/4 CUP DRY WHITE WINE

SERVES 4

❖ Grind all spices together in a spice grinder or food processor. Use 1 1/2 tbsp Spice Mixture per 1 lb peeled prawns (21 to 25 per pound).

❖ Melt 1/2 of the butter in a sauté pan. Add garlic and prawns. Add 1 1/2 tbsp Spice Mixture and brown lightly. Add beer, white wine, and Worchestershire sauce. Simmer until prawns are cooked (approximately 2 to 3 minutes). Swirl in remaining butter.

Seasonal Greens with Spiced Pecans, Gorgonzola, and Sherry Vinaigrette

1/2 LB MESCULIN GREENS MIXTURE
1/4 CUP SHERRY VINAIGRETTE DRESSING
4 OZ GORGONZOLA CHEESE
20 CANDIED PECANS

❖ SHERRY VINAIGRETTE

1/4 CUP SHERRY VINEGAR
1 TBSP DIJON MUSTARD
2/3 CUP OLIVE OIL
1/2 CUP WALNUT OIL
1/2 TSP SALT
1/2 TBSP FRESHLY GROUND PEPPER

❖ CANDIED PECANS

2 LB RAW PECAN HALVES
3/4 CUP BROWN SUGAR
1 TBSP SALT
2 TSP FRESHLY GROUND BLACK PEPPER
2 TSP GROUND CINNAMON
1 TSP GROUND CAYENNE
1 TSP GROUND PAPRIKA

SERVES 4

You can purchase the lettuce mix at your local grocery store. The Gorgonzola that is used by Waterfront Seafood Grill is from Italy. You can purchase your favorite gorgonzola, or ask your local cheese supplier what they recommend.

❖ Combine vinegar, mustard, salt and pepper. Slowly, drizzle in oil until all ingredients are combined.

❖ Blanch pecans in boiling water for 1 minute. Let dry for 3 minutes. Combine all dry ingredients until smooth and well blended. Toss pecans with dry ingredients. Place on a sheet pan. Roast in a 350° oven for 15 to 20 minutes until lightly browned

Ahi Piccata

1 OZ OLIVE OIL

1 8 OZ PORTION OF AHI STEAK

2 TBSP OF HERB MIX,
PARSLEY, ROSEMARY, THYME

1 1/2 BABY ARTICHOKES, BLANCHED

2 TSP CAPERS, DRAINED

1 TSP FRESH LEMON JUICE

3 OZ WHITE WINE

2 OZ UNSALTED BUTTER

SALT AND PEPPER TO TASTE

SERVES 1

METHOD FOR ARTICHOKES

Boil 1 quart salted water. Trim tips of artichokes and peel green layer away with a pairing knife. Trim the bottom of the artichoke and cut in half. Clean the center of the artichoke. Reserve in lemon water. Repeat process with remaining artichokes. Blanch in salted water till tender (about 8 minutes). Cool in refrigerator.

COOKING METHOD

Coat tuna with herbs, salt and pepper. Heat oil in sauté pan. Sear tuna to form a crust (light brown). Turn over and put in 500° oven until medium rare (7 to 9 minutes). Rest tuna on cutting board.

METHOD FOR SAUCE

Add 1 oz butter to sauté pan. Cook capers and artichoke hearts. Deglaze with white wine. Add lemon juice, turn heat down and start adding butter slowly until sauce emulsifies. Adjust taste with salt and pepper.

Slice tuna on diagonal. Place on plate and pour sauce around fish. Garnish with fried leeks.

Waterfront Chocolate Cake

SERVES 4

Melt chocolate and butter in doubleboiler. When melted, add brandy. Combine and cool.

In stand mixer, combine eggs, yolks, salt, sugar, and vanilla. Whip until thick and pale yellow. Fold melted chocolate mixture in by hand. Sift into mix and fold in.

Grease and flour 3" cake pan or ramekin. Fill pans 2/3 full. Scoop 1/4 oz chilled Ganache and push into middle of unbaked cakes until Ganache is no longer visible but not pushed to the bottom. Bake at 350° for 12 to 15 minutes. Cake will be soft on top and crest the pan by 1/2". As it cools, center will collapse.

❖ Melt chocolate and butter in doubleboiler. Combine cream and port wine. Heat cream and wine. Do not boil. When chocolate is melted, combine with warm cream. Pour into plastic lined bowl and refrigerate. Drizzle over cooled cake.

10 OZ CHOCOLATE
1/2 CUP BUTTER
2 TBSP BRANDY
4 EGGS
1/2 CUP SUGAR
2 TSP VANILLA
1/2 TSP SALT
3 TBSP FLOUR

❖ GANACHE
6 OZ CHOCOLATE
1/2 CUP + 1 TBSP CREAM
2 TBSP PORT WINE
1 TBSP BUTTER

❖ CRÈME ANGLAISE
1 CUP HALF AND HALF
4 EGG YOLKS
1/4 CUP SUGAR
1 TBSP HAZELNUT LIQUOR

199

❖ In a bowl, beat egg yolks and sugar. Heat half and half to a simmer in a heavy pot. Pour over egg yolk mixture while whisking. Return to pot over low flame. Stir constantly until mixture thickens enough to coat back of spoon, then add liquor. Strain through fine sieve and refrigerate.

Wine Pairing

WICKED SHRIMP
2000 MAGHIE MERLOT

SEASONAL GREENS WITH SPICED PECANS, GORGONZOLA,
AND SHERRY VINAIGRETTE
2002 KENNEDY SHAH CHENIN BLANC/VIOGNIER

AHI PICCATA
2000 DARIGHE

WATERFRONT CHOCOLATE CAKE
KENNEDY SHAH PORT

200

WOODHOUSE FAMILY CELLARS IS PRODUCING some of the best wine out of the Red Mountains and Konnowac Vinyards. Owners Bijal and Sinead Shah and Winemaker Tom Campbell, Bijal's uncle, began producing wine in 1998. Today their wines have gained such notoriety that they are becoming a premium cult-wine.

The release and sell out of the 1998 and 1999 Darighe surpassed all expectations, and continues to do so with growing excitement of future releases. Darighe is a Bordeaux blend featuring grapes from the Konnowac Vineyards, south of Yakima. The name Darighe is Gaelic for "red," appropriate for the wine's color and the passion it evokes among collectors. Each vintage is pre-allocated and released in limited quantities.

In addition to Darighe, Woodhouse Family Cellars also produces small allocations of two other wines from the Red Mountain region—Dussek, featured on a premium Cabernet Sauvignon, and Maghie, featured on a premium Merlot. The newest addition to the Woodhouse label is Kennedy Shah, named after the Shah's young daughter. This label includes a 1.5 liter Chenin Blanc/Viognier, Merlot, Cabernet Sauvignon, and a Syrah. Kennedy Shah Wine donates twenty percent of the gross revenue to women and children's charities throughout the Pacific Northwest.

Woodhouse Family Cellars is currently developing a tasting room in the Woodinville area to give wine enthusiasts a chance to taste some of the best boutique wine in Washington.

WOODHOUSE
FAMILY CELLARS

BIJAL AND SINEAD SHAH,
OWNERS

15500 WOODINVILLE-
REDMOND ROAD
SEATTLE, WA 98072
206.382.1805
www.woodhousefamilycellars.com

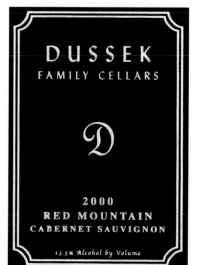

LIQUID AND DRY MEASURES

U.S.			METRIC
1/4 teaspoon			1.23 milliliters
1/2 teaspoon			2.46 milliliters
3/4 teaspoon			3.7 milliliters
1 teaspoon			4.93 milliliters
1 1/4 teaspoons			6.16 milliliters
1 1/2 teaspoons			7.39 milliliters
1 3/4 teaspoons			8.63 milliliters
2 teaspoons			9.86 milliliters
1 tablespoon			14.79 milliliters
2 tablespoons			29.57 milliliters

3 teaspoons	1 tablespoon	1/2 ounce	14.3 grams
2 tablespoons	1/8 cup	1 ounce	28.3 grams
4 tablespoons	1/4 cup	2 ounces	56.7 grams
5 1/3 tablespoons	1/3 cup	2.6 ounces	75.6 grams
8 tablespoons	1/2 cup	4 ounces	113.4 grams
12 tablespoons	3/4 cup	6 ounces	170 grams
16 tablespoons	1 cup	8 ounces	226.8 grams
32 tablespoons	2 cups	16 ounces	453.6 grams
64 tablespoons	4 cups	32 ounces	907.2 grams

1 oz.			30 milliliters
16 oz	1 pint		475 milliliters
32 oz	1 quart		950 milliliters
128 oz	1 gallon	3.75 liters	3750 milliliters

1/2 pound			252 grams
1.1 pounds			500 grams
2.2 pounds		1 kilo	1000 grams

1 lb flour	4 cups		
1 lb granulated sugar	2 cups		
1/4 lb butter	1/2 cup	1 stick	113.4 grams
1 lb butter	2 cups	4 sticks	453.6 grams

8 oz can	1 cup		226.8 grams
#1 can	1 1/4 cups		
#303 can	2 cups		453.6 grams

1 cup	1/2 pint	8 fluid ounces	237 ml
2 cups	1 pint	16 fluid ounces	474 ml
4 cups	1 quart	32 fluid ounces	948 ml
2 pints	1 quart	32 fluid ounces	948 ml
2 quarts	1/2 gallon	64 fluid ounces	1.896 liters
4 quarts	1 gallon	128 fluid ounces	3.792 liters

1 inch			0.0254 m
1 foot			0.3048 m

TEMPERATURES

DEGREES FAHRENHEIT	OVEN TEMPERATURE	DEGREES CELSIUS
250 – 300	very slow	121.11 – 148.89
300 – 325	slow	148.89 – 162.78
325 – 350	moderate	162.78 – 176.67
375	moderately hot	190.56
400 – 425	hot	204.44 – 218.33
450 +	very hot	232.22 +

NOTES